More Than Just Money

Practical and Provocative Steps to Nonprofit Success

More Than Just Money:
Practical and Provocative Steps to Nonprofit Success

Copyright © 2010 by Allen J. Proctor

The essays contained herein were originally published in *Columbus Business First* from 2006 to 2009, with changes for this edition.

Bulk orders of ten or more copies of MORE THAN JUST MONEY
may be ordered directly from:
LMM Press
471 Highgate Avenue
Worthington, OH 43085

Email info@linkingmissontomoney.com
for price and shipping information.

Cover design: Dustin Verdin
Index by Clive Pyne Book Indexing Services

Library of Congress Card Catalogue Number: 2010901845
ISBN-10: 1-450571-89-1
EAN-13: 978-1-450571-89-0

First Printing: June 2010
10 9 8 7 6 5 4 3 2 1
Printed in the United States of America

More Than Just Money

Practical and Provocative Steps to Nonprofit Success

Allen Proctor

Author of *Linking Mission to Money* ®

Foreword by **E. Gordon Gee**
President, The Ohio State University

.

To Ricky
and the family that loves him

ACKNOWLEDGMENTS

This book represents five years of thinking about what nonprofit executives and boards need to know. I want to thank Dominic Cappa for deciding that a regular column in *Columbus Business First* would be a useful way to serve nonprofit readers. The space limitations of a monthly column provided the incentive to address key nonprofit issues in the tightly focused, succinct style used in the columns and in this book.

I would also like to thank Susanne Jaffe, for her great editing and calm direction on how to bring this book to publication, and Dustin Verdin for designing the cover.

The nonprofit executives and board members I have worked with provided the grist for this book. Each chapter addresses one or more challenges they have faced. Seeing where they struggled and what factors underlay their successes highlighted the need to broadcast the message that success in the nonprofit world is not guaranteed by wealth. Success requires more than just money. The lessons in this book will help you succeed within the resources available.

TABLE OF CONTENTS

FOREWORD

This is a book that everyone involved with nonprofit organizations will find both useful and inspiring. Whether you are a staff member, a board member, or a volunteer for such an organization, you are an important stakeholder in its sustainability. *More Than Just Money* provides invaluable information, practical steps, and provocative lessons to increase the probability of success for your organization.

I have had the privilege of working with Allen Proctor on several significant projects at Ohio State. He has the unique ability to take the complicated, even arcane, and make it cogent, understandable, and achievable. He is known as a talented financial professional who believes deeply that success, especially with a nonprofit, is about more than money. It is also about working to ameliorate some of society's most vexing problems. As Allen writes, "There is merit to feeding the hungry, helping troubled youth, housing the homeless, tutoring a child, producing art, and making music." And that is the intrinsic value of this book: its perspective on all aspects of good nonprofit management, not just fiscal.

Professor Jeremy Knowles, the late Dean of the Faculty of Arts and Sciences at Harvard University, said this of Allen Proctor's first book, *Linking Mission to Money*®*:*

"Proctor's demystifying book is important, and he argues powerfully that while budgets, projections, and fiscal prudence are essential, we must never forget the higher aspirations of our institutions."

Allen's columns on nonprofit management have appeared in such publications as *Business First,* and I always read them eagerly. They provide insight on a variety of issues that university presidents, board chairs, and chief executives of nonprofits grapple with each day. *More Than Just Money* presents a similar approach: concise, easy-to-read chapters on subjects ranging from board governance and endowment management to sustaining donor relationships, maintaining missions through financial crises, and much more.

As the president of a comprehensive public research university, I found the chapters on philanthropy particularly provocative. In that section, Allen describes the pressing need for leaders of nonprofits to help donors understand that unrestricted gifts carry more power to advance missions and priorities than do narrowly defined gifts. It is this kind of common sense approach that makes the book particularly useful to all of us who work in service to the greater good.

E. Gordon Gee
President
The Ohio State University

INTRODUCTION

There were 276,101 charitable organizations that reported to the Internal Revenue Service in 2004. They held assets of $2 trillion and had revenues of $1.2 trillion. Contributions accounted for only one-fifth of their revenues, a share that has shown little change for the last quarter century. And investment earnings have never exceeded five percent over that period. Rather, these organizations supported their services by selling: earning revenues through such means as admissions, fees, charges, and memberships.

While these figures sound like a for-profit business that is doing well, those who manage and govern nonprofits know that 2004 was just another year in a period of seemingly perpetual stress. One way to illustrate this stress is the National Arts Index of the health and vitality of the nonprofit arts in the United States. This index peaked in 1999, hit a low in 2002, and recovered slightly only to establish a new low as the next recession began in 2008. A broader measure of stress is net income for the entire nonprofit sector in the United States. Net income also peaked in 1999 and, in the subsequent recession, plunged 75 percent to a 20-year low. It took five years for nonprofits to get net income back to 1999 levels. Yet it would be a mistake to attribute this stress to failed fundraising or ineffective marketing: IRS data for 1985-2004 show no year in which earned income or contributions declined.

This conundrum that continuous growth of earnings and contributions has not insulated the nonprofit sector from severe financial stress is the motivation for this book. While critics urge nonprofits to increase charges or boost their fundraising in order to get out of a recessionary crisis, past experience suggests that the solution must be found in more profound changes in how we think about nonprofits and how we manage, govern, and support them.

Nonprofit success requires more than just money. It requires an understanding of the special characteristics of effective nonprofit governance, planning, and management. Nonprofit governance requires that boards master the difficult balance between advocacy and fiduciary oversight. Nonprofit board members can be effective only when nonprofits engage and maintain the passion, commitment, and enthusiasm that brought individuals onto the board in the first place.

Effective planning is fundamental to nonprofit success because addressing nonprofit mission is a much more difficult goal than the for-profit goal of strong earnings or increasing share prices. The fundamental nonprofit mission is to be a reliable provider of a community need. This mission can be achieved only by looking ahead to anticipate change in the community and to plan how to sustain services through the ups and downs of a business cycle.

My first book, *Linking Mission to Money*®, guides board members and executives through all aspects of the nonprofit life cycle and deliberately dispels the plethora of misconceptions about what constitutes effective nonprofit management. This book goes further, probing more specifically the components of effective nonprofit management. Its underlying theme is that five factors impact the current stress in the nonprofit sector:

- An inability to figure out how to effectively use and engage boards of directors.

- Ignorance of, or just ignoring, the business cycle and its impact on nonprofit revenues and expenses.

- An overemphasis on building endowments and investment income rather than on building operating cash.

- A change in the relationship between donors and nonprofits such that the donor has become the client and the nonprofit has been demoted to being a contractor.

- A continued shift toward the nonprofit sector as the provider of key governmental services.

This book will provide you with practical, and often provocative, steps you can use for your nonprofit to succeed in this environment. Some chapters provide approaches that will challenge you to think more deeply about the underlying causes of the stresses and challenges your nonprofit faces. Other chapters provide specific tools you can use to assemble solutions to those challenges.

The chapters are meant to be read and reread to remind you and challenge you to govern, plan, and manage effectively in a deliberate, bold, and insightful manner. The Appendix provides additional reminders of what nonprofit boards and managers should be doing now to get to and stay on a path to success. And the Glossary translates the arcane into everyday language. A careful reading of this book should dispel some of the hesitation and timidity that prevent many nonprofits from exhibiting the boldness and calculated risk-taking shown by successful for-profits.

Nonprofits fulfill important needs of the community that no one else is willing or able to do. It is important and difficult work. While money is important to survival, nonprofit success is about more than just money. With this book you will have the insight and information you need to be confident in charting a course for your nonprofit that addresses your community's needs, engages a talented and committed board, and uses finance as a tool to keep your nonprofit laser-focused on fulfilling its mission.

Yours in Linking Mission to Money$^{®}$

Allen J. Proctor

More Than Just Money

Practical and Provocative Steps to Nonprofit Success

I. ROLE OF THE BOARD

During good economic times, a nonprofit can get along with a board that attends a few meetings each year and does little else. In today's economic and philanthropic environment, however, boards become the greatest strength, or the greatest weakness, of a nonprofit organization.

The nonprofits that will be successful will be the ones that figure out how to make their boards effective. The foundation for an effective board is a useful and meaningful board meeting that has a clear purpose and incorporates informed decision-making while giving board members useful work to perform between meetings. Too often nonprofits assemble a roster of talented board members but neglect the more important challenge of figuring out how to use them effectively.

The biggest barriers to effectiveness are too strong an emphasis on the number of board members and a belief that if a board can't or won't raise a lot of money, it is neither useful nor effective. Large boards can be less effective than small boards. And boards that raise a lot of money are not that common. More typically, the people who are willing to join boards do not have the potential or ability to raise large sums. But they have time, passion, knowledge, experience, and relationships, which have tremendous value to the nonprofit if it views them as resources to be routinely tapped.

The best approach to tap a board's value is to exploit its Rolodex® and its diversity of knowledge, experience, and relationships. Both can be utilized to expand the range of programs, clients, donors, outreach methods, and financial strategies beyond what the nonprofit's staff can do on their own.

When a nonprofit needs services, advice, or expertise it doesn't possess, board members should be asked if they can provide it or who they know who can provide it, possibly at no cost. All nonprofits need to broadcast how well they fulfill important community needs. This advocacy is important and routine work for every board member, especially during hard times when the perception of being important to the community can persuade the community to buy tickets, make donations, or volunteer more time. It is important to match nonprofit's needs with the skills and passion of each board member.

There are helpful warning signs to use to assess if you have the right board members — talented people who are engaged, committed, and available. Engaged so they feel connected to the organization. Committed so they see advocacy and fundraising as essential board duties. Available so they attend enough meetings and key events to make their talents and advocacy beneficial to the organization. Key to assessing the effectiveness of a board is setting clear and realistic expectations and regularly evaluating the performance and engagement of each board member.

■ The Board and the Budget

When many nonprofits begin to develop budgets for the following year, reams of paper will be copied, tables of numbers will stare out defiantly, a few questions will be asked, and a budget will be approved by the board.

Some boards will take out a magnifying glass and drill the staff for hours on every line in the budget, from office supply expenses to increases in health-care benefits. Other boards go to the opposite extreme, devoting 15 minutes to a short staff presentation before asking for a vote to approve.

As with most things in life, the right balance lies in between. That balance is a narrow but intense focus on three decisions:

- Should the organization do anything next year that is different from what it is doing this year?

- How is the organization going to balance the budget for next year if it does choose to do things differently?

- What should the organization do in times of economic crisis if it does not allow a deficit budget to be passed?

An effective budget process provides to the board only those details relevant to decisions the board needs to be involved in. Everything else the board should leave to the staff.

Unfortunately for most boards, the process, whether it lasts 15 minutes or 15 days, fails to dig deeply into the first decision. I suspect this is because too little thought has been devoted to what a board is supposed to do with a budget.

Budget distractions

Don't make the mistake of thinking of the budget as just an exercise in adding up expenses and revenue and making sure they balance.

Imagine the organization is an automobile and the board is the driver. Mission and community need represent the steering wheel, determining the path the organization will take. Finance represents the brake and accelerator pedals, determining how fast the organization travels along that path. The board's first focus in the budget process should be the steering wheel; that is, how it plans to meet the needs of the community and sustain its mission.

Strategic planning is the tool most boards use to steer. The budget is useful and relevant only to the extent that it links actions and resources with the strategy and with the change the strategy requires. The budget process creates that linkage by laying out clearly how, what, and when changes will occur over the coming year.

So the budget is about finances only at the most superficial level. The budget is mostly a decision concerning how staff will spend their time, how well the organization can absorb change, and how successfully the organization believes it can modify some ongoing activities in order to accommodate new ones.

Most budget detail is not germane to these decisions. At the staff level, there are myriad details that must be examined, but such details can distract the board from its strategic focus.

The technique and complexity of the approach to budget building is less important than the objective of building a budget: To identify priorities and have an affordable plan of action that the board can follow over a 12-month period that will achieve those priorities by the end of the budget year. The ideal budget process from a board perspective is one that keeps the board's focus on strategic decisions.

Strategic view

In working with my clients I have found that this is most effectively accomplished by utilizing an approach that I call continuation and initiative budgeting. This approach separates information on continuing, unchanging activities from information on the special efforts that are being proposed to advance or modify delivery of the mission.

This approach can allow the board to focus on whether it wishes to advance or modify the mission and whether the special efforts are financially or programmatically desirable.

Board deliberation on the budget should focus almost entirely on the initiatives, on the choice to run a surplus or a deficit or to be exactly in balance, and on the method to finance the deficit or set aside the surplus. These board deliberations may conclude that the number or size of the initiatives needs to be adjusted, reserves need to be modified, a few ongoing activities need to be scaled back, some ongoing revenue needs to be expanded, or any variation on the above.

The board's greatest value is its strategic perspective from 10,000 feet up. The appeal of the continuation and initiative approach to budgeting is that it makes it much easier for the board to apply its strategic perspective to reviewing a budget.

If a board has a good sense of its mission, goals, and priorities, this approach is worth testing for the next budget round.

In his book *Peter Drucker on the profession of management*, Drucker observed that the best nonprofits have advantages over for-profit businesses through their focus on mission and their effective use of their boards of directors. What, specifically, should nonprofit boards to do be effective?

Effectiveness must be evaluated against purpose. The purpose of the board should be to ensure that the nonprofit can reliably serve a need in the community.

Here is a checklist of what your board can do to be effective. The recommendations fall into three categories: defining the purpose of the board; focusing on the future, not on the past; and aligning fundraising with the priorities of your organization's mission.

Define your job and stick to it

Any job worth doing has a description of key duties and expected outcomes.

Have written expectations for each board member for attendance at meetings and key events, personal giving, and advocacy and outreach on behalf of the organization. Each board member should be evaluated annually against these duties and outcomes.

Each committee should have a charter that describes its role and key annual tasks and decisions, which should be coordinated with board decision-making. Each committee should be evaluated annually on its performance.

Every meeting should have a purpose

Meetings are the most visible aspect of a board's work.

Create a timetable of topics for your board meetings over the next year that maintains a continual board focus on identification and advancement of long-term goals.

Prepare your meeting agendas so that the purpose and intended outcomes of the meeting are clear and the focus is on discussion and decision-making. Informational presentations should be minimized.

Board materials, including the agenda, should be distributed at least one week in advance and should be clearly focused on items for discussion and decision.

Discussions look forward, not backward

A board sets strategic direction and oversees compliance with that strategy. This requires that board time and effort be forward-looking and focused on adjustments needed to maintain mission priorities.

Put in place a process to review at least every two years how the community's needs have changed and how your service programs and mission should adapt in response to the changes.

Determine how sensitive your nonprofit is to the health of the economy and make sure that you have at least one goal or objective each year that enhances the future sustainability of your services. Identify your need for working capital and your need for separate reserves for emergencies, new program development, and major replacement costs. Have a plan to address those needs over the next five to 10 years and follow it.

- Create a summary of what you are doing this year to move toward your long-term goals. Regularly communicate this to board members, staff, donors, clients, and patrons.

- Identify the three to five primary activities of your organization and estimate the principal revenues, contributions, and expenses for each activity. Make sure the activities with lower mission priorities have either smaller financial losses or larger net revenues.

- Set up a process to verify throughout the year that spending remains consistent with the priorities the board has set for the year. Ask as many questions about underspending as you ask about overspending. Underspending can reflect under-performance, which is not an appropriate way to save money. Make sure you don't have cost savings that may be undermining the mission-effectiveness of your programs.

Fundraising sustains mission

The board is responsible for assuring that adequate resources are available to sustain mission. Fundraising should serve mission, and the board must be vigilant that the way money is raised does not limit flexibility in meeting mission priorities.

- Identify any restrictions on gifts and assets and compare them to your top mission priorities. Take steps to prevent restrictions from diverting your nonprofit's activities from its top mission priorities.

- Make sure that your fundraising focuses on sustainability by first building unrestricted cash and reserves to adequate levels before focusing on endowment.

- Always have a tickler schedule for when you expect to receive payments on major pledges and grants and have the board intercede whenever receipts are delayed.

- Know what are your unrestricted net assets and whether they are board designated, fixed, or readily spendable for any purpose. Know how or whether each of the assets can be used to pay your bills that are due this year.

- Require that any proposal to expand facilities or services specify how the expansion and its future operating costs will be supported from new or expanded revenue sources.

Taking each of these steps will improve the effectiveness of your board. The reward will be engaged board members who have purposeful meetings that strengthen the sustainability and relevance of your mission.

■ The Right Board Members

A nonprofit thrives when it has a board of directors that is committed to its success.

Such a board is comprised of people who are able to provide three critical attributes:

- A personal passion for the mission and role of the nonprofit organization.

- A commitment to work for the success of the organization by providing time, financial support, and public advocacy.

- The ability to free up sufficient time to be active and involved in all leadership activities of the organization.

Look for three warning signs that the board is missing some of these attributes: Attendance is so poor they struggle to have quorums at meetings; participation is so poor that few board members can be seen at events, performances, and openings; and financial support is so poor that few board members' names appear in the top categories of donors.

Board participation and involvement are also public evidence that board members are exercising their fiduciary duty to support and sustain the mission of the nonprofit organization. That participation is viewed by donors, patrons, and staff as a demonstration of the board's loyalty and commitment to the nonprofit organization.

At a performance or opening celebration of a new program, for instance, all the board members are expected to attend, and similarly at a fundraiser. The majority are expected to be on the list of major donors.

When a board struggles with board participation and commitment, it needs to put board restructuring at the top of its agenda and consider the possibility that an entirely different board must be recruited.

The first place to start is to establish expectations.

A successful nonprofit board sets high expectations for itself and each of its members. This is done several ways:

- Recruit members to provide specific critical attributes and skills that are needed by the nonprofit. Many organizations create a grid of key skills, relationships, and interests, and try to have each item provided by at least one board member.

- Document in writing what is expected of each board member. Some boards use a written contract which details the expectations for the board member and for the organization.

- Annually review board members' performance and meet with each board member to assess his or her continuing interest in board membership and terms of service.

- Choose a chair (and chair-elect) that is able and willing to demonstrate leadership in all key areas: philanthropy, board service, and attendance at programs and events.

Finding the Right People

Typically, the board will have a nominating or governance committee. Ideally, this committee should have a written charter that assigns it five broad duties that go far in creating the right board to lead the nonprofit organization toward success:

1. Board Role and Responsibilities

- Leads the board in regularly reviewing and updating the board's role and areas of responsibility, and the expectations of individual board members.

- Assists the board in periodically updating and clarifying the primary areas of focus for the board for the next year or two, based on the strategic plan.

2. Board Composition

- Leads in assessing needs for board composition, determining the board's knowledge, attributes, skills, abilities, influence, and access the board will need to consider in order to accomplish future work.

- Identifies and nominates potential board member candidates and explores with each candidate his or her interest in and availability for board service.

- Meets annually with each board member to assess his or her continuing interest in board membership and term of service. Works with each board member to identify the appropriate role he or she might assume on behalf of the organization.

3. Board Knowledge

- Designs and oversees a process of board orientation and implements an ongoing program of board information and education for all board members.

4. Board Effectiveness

- Leads the periodic assessment of the board's performance; proposes changes in board structure, roles, and responsibilities when it's appropriate.

- Regularly reviews the board's practices regarding member participation, financial contribution, conflict of interest, confidentiality, and suggests improvements as needed.

5. Board Leadership

- Takes the lead in succession planning, taking steps to recruit and prepare for future board leadership.

- Nominates board members for election as board officers.

■ Realistic Goals for the Board

A provocative question is how can boards spearhead development of an effective strategy.

This question brought to mind *Governance as Leadership, Reframing the Work of Nonprofit Boards,* by Richard Chait, a highly regarded Harvard professor. The book challenges what it is we want boards to do. Chait asks, "Why do nonprofit(s) go to such great lengths to recruit the best and brightest as trustees but then permit these stalwarts to languish collectively in an environment more intellectually inert than alive?"

Chait starts with three reasons why a nonprofit should want to have a board.

First, a nonprofit acquires legitimacy by recruiting board members who are respected in the community.

Second, a board meeting provides a deadline for management to pull together a sensible and coherent account of how and what the organization is doing.

Third, a board provides an incentive for managers to attend to their duties.

While these are good reasons for having a board, they are not very compelling reasons for becoming a board member. To address this, Chait delves into how a board can appeal to a board member.

The fiduciary duties of a board are essential. The board must ensure money is used properly, mission is the focus of effort, and services are effective and in compliance with laws and regulations. Chait cautions against overemphasizing this role because meetings become overly narrow, and "the board develops such a limited sense of the organization that the board's ability to challenge and enrich organizational thinking atrophies."

The strategic duties of a board are essential, particularly in fostering a dialogue on new concepts. The board must not leave this up to the chief executive, Chait argues, because abdicating the mandating and monitoring of a strategic plan deprives the board of a key governing role and deprives board members of being engaged.

 Chait criticizes boards that focus on how to get to a goal rather than on what the goal is and why it is important.

"Boards are better suited to think together than plan together, to expand the essence of a great idea rather than elaborate the details of a plan."

Boards should pose fundamental questions, Chait says, such as:

- What will be the consequences to this university now that others have made knowledge free on the Web?

- Can we flourish in a neighborhood in decline? If not, do we relocate?

- Is the business model of this and other performing arts organizations viable over the next 20 years? If not, what has to change?

To emphasize this point, Chait coins a new term: generative governing. By this he means governing that focuses on thinking and making sense of the past, present, and future of the organization. A board does this by questioning assumptions, probing feasibility of activities, and identifying obstacles and opportunities. This corrals the power of a diverse board to use their multiple perspectives for disciplined thinking to develop strategy.

Chait challenges us to question the structure of our board meetings. Rather than fixed agendas with presentations and votes, he urges board meetings to become discussions of fundamental issues, in many ways adopting the tone of board retreats for a portion of every board meeting. Ideally, the board meeting needs to maintain balance among all three roles: fiduciary oversight, strategy formulation, and open-ended thinking.

The value of Chait's book is his challenge to us to make our boards into thinking boards that consider questions such as how we have succeeded in the past and why; what is happening in our industry and will that strengthen us or challenge us; what was the community need that brought us into existence and how has it and will it change? If we can do this, the board will have an effective way to spearhead development of a strategy.

■ Engaging the Board

Nonprofits thrive when their boards are engaged and actively committed.

How well that is achieved is determined by what happens at board meetings. An effective board meeting can create commitment and engage each board member in advancing the mission that attracted them to the board in the first place.

There are four keys to structuring an effective board meeting that encourages attendance, engagement, and active commitment by all members of the board.

The first key is a clear understanding of the board's role and the purpose of conducting meetings. The primary role of a board is to ensure performance of mission, provide adequate financial and nonfinancial resources for the mission to be achievable, and exercise financial stewardship that resources are being used effectively and responsibly.

The purpose for having any board meeting should be for the board to carry out those roles.

More on the checklist

The second key is to use the meeting agenda to clearly indicate what decisions will be made and what outcomes are expected. Ask yourself three questions whenever you see an agenda:

- What is the purpose of the meeting as described by the topics on the agenda?

- What do you expect will be the main accomplishment of the meeting?

- Could a board member prepare in advance for this meeting?

If you see report after report on the agenda, you may be sending board members an unintended message — that the purpose of the meeting is to hear a recital from management and no major discussion will occur and no decisions will be made.

The third key is to structure meetings in ways that counter the following four obstacles to board attendance, engagement and active commitment:

- Board members are unpaid volunteers who have four to 12 board meetings a year in which to fulfill their roles. This time needs to be highly productive or they will never feel engaged with the organization.

- A quality board wants serious work to do. Many board members will feel peripheral or undervalued and will disengage when too many decisions and discussions are closely held by the chair or take place in an executive committee.

- Good board members have dozens of demands on their time. A board meeting that has a vague or poorly articulated purpose does not compete well with other time demands when the board member asks "Does it matter if I attend or not?"

- Good board members are decision-makers who like to be prepared. They become uncomfortable and distance themselves when cast in the role of hearing reports rather than as participating in meaningful discussions and decisions. Materials must be sent in advance that allow board members to arrive prepared to make sound decisions.

The fourth key is to think of each meeting as an opportunity for each board member to participate usefully in one or more of the following ways.

- Ask questions that seek to link mission to money.

- Flag issues critical to mission sustainability.

- Provide advice and support on issues to be addressed in subsequent board meetings.

Setting the program

An agenda that effectively allows board members to be active participants has three parts:

1. Operating status: A brief review of a handful of financial and non-financial measures key to the organization. Identify four to six measures that can identify emergence of problems and flag the need for more extensive board discussion.

2. Follow up on board assignments from the last meeting: An engaged board member leaves a meeting with something to do. Following up on progress each meeting reminds board members that what they are asked to do is important and valued.

3. Review status of priorities and assign actions to be accomplished by the next meeting. An organization has dozens of activities but only a few priorities. Board time should be focused on the priorities and on identifying assignments for board members that advance those priorities.

Take a look at the agendas for your last few board meetings. Did they prompt advice and decisions that sustained and fostered the mission of the organization? Did board members feel their attendance was important to the organization?

If you answered no to either question, then revisit the purpose of your board meetings and how you structure your agendas. Once you do, you may find a higher level of engagement, better attendance, and more active participation that make your board the one people want to join.

■ Evaluating the Board

As you consider the characteristics you need from new board candidates, it is a good time to take a hard look at your board's profile. Particularly, what is the culture of the board you are asking them to join and is it a help or a hindrance to the effectiveness and sustainability of your nonprofit organization? Culture is the tone and nature of board interrelationships as typified by the following questions. Are board members expected to socialize outside the board room? Are challenging questions encouraged or frowned upon? Are new members expected to defer to existing members? Are board meetings informational, leaving key decisions to be made by an executive committee?

Your board has worked hard over the years to assemble a membership that brings diverse skills and perspectives to the table. Yet diversity has value only to the extent that it is drawn upon. The structure of meetings and the tone of discussions are key determinants of how that diversity is utilized.

Board meetings frequently have little informed discussion. Agendas can be filled with endless presentations, brief committee reports and votes that are mere formalities. And, unfortunately, some boards may frown on members who ask questions and "slow down the meeting."

The ideal culture of a nonprofit board is one of supportive inquiry and openness. It welcomes questions, values diversity of opinion and constructive disagreement, and insists the tone and substance of meetings convey support and a keen desire to assist management.

This culture does not come without watchful attention. In fact, human nature is often its foil.

Sharp contrasts

Jim Collins, author of the well-known book *Good to Great* applied his successful techniques to the nonprofit sector and found some adjustments were necessary in order to implement his framework. His findings are published in a short monograph *Good to Great and the Social Sectors* (his term for the nonprofit sector). Let me loosely quote two entries from his summary of differences between the business sector and the nonprofit sector:

- In the business sector, he sees that "competitive market pressures force failing businesses to confront the brutal facts." In contrast, in the nonprofit sector, he sees instead a tendency toward a "culture of 'niceness' that inhibits candor about the brutal facts."

- In the business sector, he sees that "the profit mechanism makes it easier to say 'no' or to stop doing (something that doesn't) fit ... ." In contrast, in the nonprofit sector, he sees instead that a "desire to 'do good' and the personal desires of donors and funders can (cause undisciplined decision-making)."

It is important to remind ourselves that the same type of people occupy both business and nonprofit board seats, yet Collins sees that the different cultures of those sectors can lead to different behaviors by board members unless a conscious effort is made to counter the less desirable differences.

Collins' observations are not a surprise to anyone who has worked in the nonprofit sector. What is refreshing is that such a visible advocate of excellence has openly acknowledged that good intentions can have very different consequences in a business board room than in a nonprofit board room.

But tendencies don't have to lead to outcomes. It is important that nonprofit boards take Collins' cue and acknowledge that good boards in the nonprofit sector require a proactive discipline that his "market forces" tend to impose automatically on a business board.

Engaging the board

I serve on both business and nonprofit boards and I see this difference at every meeting. There are many good, even great, nonprofit boards, but they constantly must work at it and vigilantly counter any tendency to ignore, excuse, or foster poor decision-making.

I urge you to consciously examine the culture of your board to see if it encourages questions, values diverse perspectives, and readily tackles challenging issues.

- Do you see board members who say nothing during a meeting?

- Do you ensure that each member's opinions are known and that each member has a sufficient understanding of the issue at hand and its importance to the organization?

- Do you actively seek out board members' doubts, concerns, or worries about a strategy, policy, or course of action?

Define a successful board culture as one that puts existing or emerging problems on the table for open discussion and resolution. Scan board members' eyes during a meeting to see where confusion or concern may appear and be sure no board member still has that look by the time the meeting ends.

If you do this, the board will be more engaged, it will view each meeting as an opportunity to make a positive contribution, the staff will regard each board meeting as an opportunity for problems to be solved, and your non-profit can move from good to great.

II. THE EXECUTIVE DIRECTOR

The executive director, president, or CEO, as the principal administrator of a nonprofit, must manage up to the board and down to the staff. This is a challenging balancing act that becomes even more important during periods of crisis and change.

Focusing on pleasing the board while neglecting to effectively manage the staff will lead to failure of the organization even if the executive director manages a long tenure. Similarly, focusing on managing the staff while neglecting to ensure that the board supports the strategic direction the executive director has set will lead to a very short tenure for the executive director.

In managing staff, it is vital that the executive director learns to see the forest while developing tools to make sure the staff are minding the trees. Too often executive directors neglect simplicity in favor of a love of detail. This is a mistake that will inhibit the executive director's ability to lead effectively and strategically. Learning the right questions to ask becomes the best tool for executive directors to isolate only that detail that is essential to setting strategy and ensuring it is being effectively and appropriately implemented by staff.

In managing the board, the most difficult issue will always be making sure the board understands and supports the need for change. Community need is constantly changing and the successful nonprofit will be continually adapting its mission and strategy to those changes. Not all board members will be immediately convinced the need has changed or that the mission and strategy must change. An executive director who neglects to keep the majority of the board focused on the case for continual change will jeopardize the organization and possibly his job. Neither being a good manager nor having strong personal relationships with board members can compensate.

Balancing the needs of the board and staff with the needs of the organization and community is the heart of an executive director's job. That balance is found when perspective is more important than detail; why and where is more important than how and when; and accepting the challenge of fostering change is more important than seeking the safety of the status quo.

■ Financial Statements and What They Don't Tell

Repeated crises and scandals in the public and private sectors continue to place heavy focus on the adequacy of financial statements and the effectiveness of auditors in identifying problems.

While good should certainly come from this focus, the public discussion is raising false expectations that more auditors and better audited financial statements will make boards effective and avoid disasters.

These expectations cannot be met for a simple reason: Financial statements are based on generally accepted accounting principles, which represent a complex and sophisticated system for estimating the financial condition of an organization. An informed board of directors needs far more than complex estimates of condition. It needs reports that tell it in straightforward terms about future risks and timely execution of priorities.

Aside from outright fraud, I believe most organizational failures have at least one of the following causes:

- Inadequate focus on priorities.

- Poor execution.

- Failure to pay critical bills on time.

- Unanticipated cash shortages.

There are straightforward ways to stay on top of these issues, but financial statements will not easily yield that information. The typical financial report a board receives consists of the three financial statements required under Generally Accepted Accounting Principles (GAAP) – a balance sheet, an income statement and a cash reconciliation. These tables are not designed to address these four major causes of failure.

Ringing the alarm

Daily management is often a series of interruptions and back-to-back meetings. The press of immediate demands can easily sidetrack management from higher-level strategic issues and from the long-term priorities needed to achieve that strategy. The board, by its more periodic and strategic attention to the organization, can in many circumstances be better equipped to maintain focus on strategy and priorities than the operationally focused staff. Financial statements have limited value on this front.

Every project has its ups and downs. Slippage in key programs can be subtle but ultimately disastrous when it harms constituents, misleads donors, violates grant requirements, or erodes goodwill. A board needs a process to ring alarms when slips start to accumulate so the board can authorize changes in priorities, resources, or commitments in a way that help the staff to keep the highest priorities on track. Unless slips create significant changes in revenue or expenses, financial statements will not be a reliable ringer of alarm bells.

Juggling which bills to pay and when to pay them is the name of the game for many finance officers. Putting off paying some bills in order to pay the most vocal vendors can be disastrous when the unpaid bills are to the insurance company, retirement plan, or IRS.

Having some bills hang over from the previous month is routine, and financial statements report this well. Unfortunately, financial statements don't generally distinguish between a bill that is unpaid for two weeks versus one that is unpaid for two months, nor does the typical financial statement tell you if the unpaid bill is to the IRS, the power company, or just the local office supply store.

The tripwire of crisis is running out of cash. Every month you need to know the amount of cash that will be readily available for the next few months and what future events could potentially compromise your solvency if they didn't occur as planned. The snapshot nature and accrual focus of financial statements aren't well suited to answering these forward-looking questions.

What to ask for

To be on top of these critical issues, the well-informed board will ask for these four reports:

- The knowledge that your CEO's focus is on the highest priorities should come from a monthly narrative report on the CEO's activities.

- The knowledge that the top priority projects are on track can also come from a monthly narrative report that describes recent progress on those projects and is accompanied by a brief table showing year-to-date revenue from and expenses for each project compared with what the project had planned.

- The knowledge about the organization's unpaid bills can come partially from an accrual statement, but the board should also receive a monthly table listing all major unpaid bills and highlighting any bills unpaid for over 45 days and to whom they are due.

- The knowledge of your cash situation can come partially from the cash financial statement, but the board should also receive a cash projection for the next three or four months with a commentary on any major sales, grants, gifts, or payments that are expected in those months. The best way to be on top of this issue is to prepare your budget on a cash basis and report monthly revenue and expenses to the board on a cash basis.

An effective board receives all the information it needs in a form that is easiest for all its members to use and understand. The four reports are more useful to the board and easier to understand than conventional financial statements.

A board will not be remiss if it leaves the complexity of accrual financial statements to the staff and, if the board is large enough, to the finance and audit committees.

■ Budget Questions

An organization makes many decisions during the year that require its budget provide a reliable road map of how activities, revenue, and expenses are expected to play out.

Just as a cartographer rechecks his maps against satellite photos and a scientist regularly recalibrates his instruments, it is important that an organization recheck its budget against what happened.

The annual audit review is an excellent way to recheck the quality of your budget because it provides a systematic review of outcomes, reports, and procedures. Unfortunately, too few organizations use the audit review to do this. That is a mistake.

The first thing you should do is to double check that your budget reports and your audited statements are using the same categories and the same cash or accrual basis of accounting.

Next, ask the finance staff the following questions:

- **In what ways did the predictions in our monthly budget reports (how we expected to end the year) differ from where we ended up (this audit)?**

Use the audit to see how well your budget reports were telling you how the year was going to conclude.

Your audited reports tell you how much revenue and expenses grew the past year. What did last year's budget predict?

Near the close of the year you received budget reports forecasting how the year would end. Were those reports on the mark? If not, why not? Does the audit include some new revenue or expenses that were not anticipated in the budget reports? If that was the case, are you satisfied with the decision process that introduced those new revenue or expenses?

- **What information does the audit contain that indicates a need to change this year's budget?**

Use the audit to see if your budget is leaving out important activities or using assumptions that are no longer realistic. One of the most common discoveries is that entire categories of revenue or expenses are "off-budget." Common exclusions are investment gains and losses, use of reserves or fund balances, activities funded by restricted grants and capital campaign revenue and expenses. Make sure you know what is excluded and that the entire board is comfortable with the implications of using a partial budget. It is also a good time to double check whether your budget assumptions are realistic.

If the final results show assumptions about growth in revenue, gifts, cost of materials and outside services, health-care costs, yields on pledges, and other key factors in last year's budget were off, you must re-examine your current-year budget assumptions to be sure you won't repeat the same mistakes.

- **What storm clouds could be on the horizon?**

While you are examining the results for the past year, you should re-evaluate your vulnerability to bad luck in the coming months.

Look at your audit's operating results (revenue less expenditures) before one-time credits or charges, borrowing, use of endowments, or exceptional gifts. If this adjustment reveals a minimal surplus or a deficit, then you have little cushion against adverse developments. That means you should re-evaluate how well you can respond to crisis.

For example, if the budget erodes during the year, do you have enough assets that you can convert to cash to pay all debts and obligations that come due this year? Does it normally take more than 30 to 45 days to collect on invoices and pledges?

If so, at what point do you determine that you won't receive the payments and write them off?

The annual review of your audited financial statements is an ideal time to recalibrate your organization's budget by asking where it is most vulnerable and how effectively the budget is guiding managers and directors through the year.

If people in the organization ask why you have to have an audit meeting, ask them these three questions. If they can't provide answers, tell them why the meeting would be worth their while.

■ A Manager's Tool Kit

As a manager moves up in an organization, the job becomes less focused on daily operations and more focused on strategic direction, effective execution, and integration across all units of the organization.

This removal from the familiar operational role of previous jobs makes it essential that a manager develop tools to evaluate risk, identify weak points, and usefully support key initiatives without micromanaging. At the top of an organization, asking the right questions becomes the dominant tool to manage effectively.

Questions to ask in developing a strategic plan and budget. When developing your budget and reviewing your multi-year financial plan, you should actively review your mission, priorities, and management and financial capacities. If you are considering an expansion in program, facilities or staff, begin by asking:

- How would we change our operations to handle this expansion? Who on your staff would be affected and what is their view?

- If we hope to receive additional outside funding, have we discussed our expansion with potential donors or investors and have they assured us of additional support for the foreseeable future?

Questions to ask to achieve an engaged and effective board. A board that governs well is an asset. The executive director should regularly ask these questions to assure he is engaging all board members to fulfill their duties effectively:

- Do you see board members who say nothing during a meeting?

- Do you ensure that each member's opinions are known and that each member has a sufficient understanding of the issue at hand and its importance to the organization?

Questions to ask to improve your financial management.
One of the most difficult challenges in financial management is to focus on sufficient information to be thorough and strategic without being drawn into insignificant and distracting detail. Regularly ask:

- Can we convincingly prove that our spending reflects our priorities?

- What events might force us to deviate from delivering on our priorities this year and next?

Questions to ask when you become aware of a crisis.
A major financial crisis can emerge from a revenue forecast that was off the mark, a grant or contract that was not renewed, a significant tax assessment, or perhaps embezzlement. Start with these questions to help you to respond quickly and constructively to a financial crisis:

- Since it is prudent to expect to encounter more problems, have you established a process that will allow the staff and board to spot new and emerging problems as quickly as possible?

- Have you instituted changes in reporting and governance so that your ability to anticipate problems and respond in the early stages will be stronger next time?

Questions an audit committee should ask.

The annual audit is where the rubber meets the road for accountability, accuracy, and reliability of financial and management information. The board should develop a portfolio of questions that it routinely asks over the course of every year.

- How much cash are we supposed to have on hand? What is our action plan if cash falls below that level?

- Is there anything now or in the next year that would lead an outside auditor to have serious concerns about the health or viability of the organization?

Questions to ask in planning a campaign.
As part of any feasibility study for a major campaign, or even for annual fundraising planning, it is important to verify that the multi-year financial plan for your organization remains valid and relevant. Start by asking these questions to be sure of the financial context that your fundraising plan must complement:

- Is service demand likely to grow in future years? Will current grant and philanthropic efforts be adequate to support such growth? What does the proposed budget do to back those efforts?

- Will the level of service delivery or financial condition resulting from this budget encourage or discourage donors and grantors in providing the level of gifts anticipated in the budget and plan?

Start building your management tool kit with these questions. If you already have a tool kit, continually add to it.

■ Involvement of Staff

At a workshop I was asked whether staff should be allowed to attend a nonprofit agency's board meetings. My answer was yes.

A well-run board meeting with a focused purpose is a very time-efficient way for staff to know the priorities, challenges, and strategies of an organization. Purposeful board meetings are an important forum for discussions of emerging problems. Staffers have staked their jobs and livelihoods on the success of the organization. One can make a good argument that they deserve to know what's going on more than the board does.

Rather than make staff rely on rumor and hallway gossip, let them into the board room to see how issues are confronted, resources allocated, priorities set, and the organization's future charted. If you worry that hearing discussions of problems will discourage the staff, you can be sure the rumor mill will go well beyond what the facts warrant.

Providing minutes of a board meeting does not substitute for attendance at the meeting. Minutes are usually dry and concise, rarely conveying tone and emphasis. On the other hand, board briefing materials are often the best and most accessible written summaries of the organization's priorities and challenges. Consider giving staff access to all but the most sensitive documents.

Seeing is believing

You should not assume staff knows as much about the organization's mission, priorities, and financial health as the board does. It is also quite possible a positive, attainable, strategic perspective is hard for staff to embrace when their daily experiences confront them with the warts of the organization – limitless demands for service, inadequate resources, and unfulfilled plans to raise quality. They want to believe they are getting as much support as possible; they want to believe the board is as committed as they are. Let them see that commitment firsthand.

It is also important to acknowledge that allowing the board to be a mysterious body of strangers induces some staff to vest a magical power in the board that does not exist. This can create unrealistic staff expectations that, if the board were to know about a problem, it has the ability to set all things right.

Boards can only inspire, support, and oversee; staff must not abdicate its responsibility to communicate, manage, and solve problems. Seeing the board in action restores the board to its proper status as concerned and skilled volunteers, but mere human beings.

A few important guidelines

If staffers don't already attend board meetings, establish a few guidelines so expectations are realistic. Consider:

- This is a board meeting, not a staff meeting. Staff shouldn't outnumber board members. The board table is for board members.

Staff should sit on the perimeter unless they are participants or the table can comfortably accommodate everyone.

- Staff attendance is a privilege, not a right.

If it is a large staff, consider routinely inviting only top officers. Make an invitation a special reward offered occasionally to junior staff. Don't underestimate how powerful an incentive this can be for your most motivated staff.

- Staff are invited as observers, not as participants unless they are specifically called upon or asked to make a presentation.

This is a time for board deliberation that staffers need to respect. At the same time, as firsthand observers of board deliberations, the staff who attend can be effective communicators to other staff, especially if done through a post-meeting staff briefing session.

- Boards automatically are burdened with a presumption of secrecy.

The practice of inviting staff for specific portions of a meeting, or shuffling them in and out as executive sessions are repeatedly called, is counterproductive. Invitations should be extended for the entire meeting and executive sessions need to be handled carefully so they don't become a problem.

A best practice for handling executive sessions is to have one at every board meeting and to make it a routine and appropriate way to end each meeting. The board chair should also make it a practice to brief the executive director on each executive session. This approach prevents executive sessions from becoming unintended messages of crisis, distrust, or lack of confidence in the staff.

Board meetings are an important forum for board members and for staff. Treat them as an opportunity to foster a shared understanding of your strategy and priorities as well as a sense of partnership between the staff and the board.

■ Strategic Planning

I have been to many meetings in which the main topic of discussion was developing a strategic plan. For some organizations it was their first attempt at developing one, while others were busily forming committees, interviewing consultants, and setting deadlines for final reports.

One nonprofit head, who was wary of the entire exercise, sent me an article by school consultant Robert Evans that questioned the value of most strategic plans.

He had a point. I often see confusion between detailed business plans, which managers prepare, and strategic plans, which boards prepare. Don't mistake long lists of projects, dozens of pages of analysis, or elaborate timetables for a strategy.

My best advice: Keep your strategy simple. If you can't summarize your organization's strategy in 30 words or less, then it probably isn't a strategy.

Tripwires to strategy

One impediment to good strategic plans is that too often implementation takes the place of strategy, a means without a clearly stated end. Too many strategic plans, Evans complains, focus heavily on measurable outcomes with impossibly long to-do lists involving key operational areas like facilities, technology, staff recruitment, marketing, and fundraising.

While those might be predictable action areas, they do not describe a strategy. They address the "how," but a good strategy addresses the "why."

A second impediment is unrealistic ambition. At times, organizations initiate a strategic planning exercise to demonstrate that they are businesslike, have a vision, and are on a path to greatness (usually meaning get bigger).

Bigger is measurable while better is often not so easily measured. The path of least resistance is to focus on the bigger in hopes that it will lead to better: bigger facilities, bigger staff, larger service area, and a bigger planning committee to produce a bigger strategic plan document. Unless it produces quality that the community desires, ambition may ultimately undermine the organization.

The third impediment to effective strategic plans is the effort to try to make them also fulfill the roles of budgets and financial plans. A budget is an action plan for the next year. A financial plan goes further in time to tie anticipated resources to intended spending for the next three to five years. The best strategic plans, in contrast, extend beyond the financial plan to describe where you are today, where you want to be five to ten or more years from now, and why you need to make the move.

Distinguishing plans

These distinctions are best illustrated by an automobile analogy. Strategy consists of where you are today, where you want to go, and why you want to go there. Mission, vision, and changing community needs are inputs into that strategy. Your strategy is informed by knowing whether you can get there with your five passenger car, or whether you will need a 12 passenger van or a semi-trailer instead. This defines your capacity for passengers and freight, the kind of driver you will need, and the volume of gasoline your strategy may require.

The financial plan is the steering wheel that chooses the route you will follow for the next three years on the way toward that strategic destination. It identifies the resources you will need and it sketches out what you can expect to spend for food, lodging, fuel, and other expenses. It thinks about whether you need to replace the tires or have a tune-up before starting the trip and whether you need to take some money out of your bank account in order to follow that route.

The budget is the accelerator pedal and brake that determine how fast you go along that route. It takes a close look at the resources you have and the expenses you will incur to get to various points along that route and then determines how far to go in the next year.

The management plan worries about how much to pack, which suitcases to use, and where everyone will sit in the car. Boards don't get involved in this implementation.

It should be obvious from this analogy that the strategic plan does not need to be elaborate and complicated. Yet it also is obvious that without a good case for the new destination which a strategy provides, the work of a management plan, budget, or financial plan could ultimately take you somewhere you didn't want to go.

If your organization is undertaking some strategic planning, keep it simple to ensure you do end up with a strategy rather than an elaborate action plan that takes you to an unknown – and undesired – destination.

■ Leadership

We expect leadership but do we support it when its boldness confronts our comfort zones?

The Columbus Foundation has spent much time exploring leadership and how to teach and encourage it. In a survey it asked nonprofits, donors, and community leaders to define leadership. The respondents identified characteristics they looked for in leaders and actions they believe define leadership.

The survey response that caught my eye was the expectation that leaders take calculated risks. The willingness to take risk is one of the most underappreciated attributes of real leadership.

A leader must have a vision. With very few exceptions, a meaningful vision challenges the status quo. It tries something new. It responds to new demands. This is a risk.

Take the current insistence on greater transparency. Obviously a worthwhile community objective, transparency lets the broad public into a wider array of issues within a nonprofit: finances, budgets, program descriptions, compensation, benefits, board composition, program costs, corporate structure, and related organizations.

No organization can please everyone and each additional area expands the potential for inquiry, criticism, and interference. With this expands the likelihood that the leader will spend more time on public relations and less time on leading and managing the organization. This is a risk.

Leadership means adapting the organization to changing community need. The latter is often as much a perception as a fact and adaptation brings the risk that others will disagree that needs have changed or that the adaptation is appropriate. For example, many believe that the current environment calls for retrenchment in the nonprofit sector through mergers and collaborations. Experience has taught that mergers have a low likelihood of success. This is a risk.

Leadership means balancing the demand for growth with the need for sustainability. Denying services in order to build a safety net to be used during economic downturns is routinely criticized when the economy is expanding. At the same time, cutting budgets during economic downturns because money was not set aside earlier is equally criticized. Balancing the two often brings criticism at both ends. This is a risk.

Are we – as patrons, donors, board members, opinion leaders – by our actions supporting or penalizing meaningful risk-taking and true leadership? Addressing and responding to change requires courage and a willingness to take risks. While these words seem harmless, the reality is that taking meaningful risk means accepting the possibility of failure.

Failure and its relation to leadership are rarely discussed because we associate leadership with success. This is problematic if we expect leadership to result in dynamic organizations.

Expecting our leaders to bat 1,000, never slipping or failing outright, will never support risk-taking leadership. Is calculated risk defined as only choosing initiatives that are highly likely to succeed? Do we insist that success also mean that the initiative will be completed by a certain date, or meet specified criteria? Bold endeavors and significant changes in direction are not likely to survive these calculations.

The most demanding definition of a leader is a person who works hard for success but who is also willing to fail.

More bluntly, a leader is willing to risk getting fired in order to try something new or different.

It is no surprise that the average tenure of CEOs of public companies or presidents of universities has shortened to less than 10 years. Leaders in these areas must take risks in order for their organizations to thrive, and the consequence is that the risks accumulate over time to a point when they are asked to move on. Ironically, those that don't take risks and are satisfied with the status quo are often the leaders with the longest tenures.

Parker Palmer provides valuable insight on this issue of risk and leadership in his book *The Active Life*.

"Our culture's fearful obsession with results has sometimes, ironically, led us to abandon great objectives and settle for trivial and mediocre ends. The reason is simple. As long as 'effectiveness' is the ultimate standard by which we judge our actions, we will act only toward ends we are sure we can achieve. People who undertake projects of real breadth and depth are very unlikely to be 'effective,' since effectiveness is measured by short-term results….But people with small visions will win the effectiveness awards, since those projects are so insignificant that they can almost always 'succeed.'"

We must ask ourselves if we back the safe leader who makes constituents feel good, is comfortable with the current convention, and keeps the boat upright, but who never reaches for big ideas, bold change, or challenges the status quo.

Or are we willing to support a leader who bats only 300, striking out every so often but occasionally hitting a few home runs and, by his or her risks, helps some other organizations or initiatives score a few runs too?

How we answer these questions will determine whether those in charge will truly lead.

.

III. FINANCIAL MANAGEMENT

Financial management is about more than just numbers. Unfortunately, the numbers often get in the way of good management and common sense. The fascination with numbers can lead some to jump into detail that loses the forest for the twigs, while the fear of numbers can lead others to avoid financial reality until crisis emerges.

There are three fundamental questions that should underlie all financial management:

1. Does your spending reflect your mission and strategic plan?

2. How well do you stick to budget?

3. What events might compel you to deviate from delivering on plans, budget, and priorities in the near future?

The essence of strategy lies in the ability to say no. For nonprofits there are always ideas that sound interesting but diverge from your priorities or lose more money than you can afford. Your answers to the three questions will depend on how well you can say no.

Finance can be obscure and it is essential to make your finances transparent in a way that enables board and staff to understand your finances and financial options. If you find it difficult to answer the three questions, then your finances are not transparent enough.

One of the greatest benefits of transparency is the ability to understand the financial risks of your decisions and the nonprofit's capacity to respond to risk. What are your financial reserves, and are they sufficient to absorb the risks you choose? What are your personnel reserves, and are they sufficient to allow you to respond appropriately when risks materialize? If you cannot answer these questions, then your finances are not transparent enough and you must be especially wary of the risks in your budget and strategy.

In general the board sticks with strategy and the executive director handles implementation. This mix changes during financial crisis, when the fiduciary duty of the board requires it to become involved in implementation because there is suddenly more to do than any executive director can handle. This greater involvement must be an inclusive partnership and cannot be a board takeover. If you have focused on saying no and have made your finances transparent, you and your board will have a shared understanding of the risks they have taken and a shared responsibility for the consequences.

■ Five Important Lessons

Every chief finance officer worth his or her salt has a secret wish: To teach.

This isn't motivated by a desire to change careers or to guide our nation's youth into enlightenment. Rather, it is inspired by the need to remind their presidents and board members of some budget lessons that repeatedly are forgotten, often with unfortunate results.

The need for a refresher course is just as true in the largest and most prestigious universities as it is in a small social service agency. To test this point, I informally surveyed the chief financial officers at some universities to find out the lessons they wanted to teach their deans or presidents.

The lessons they picked may be familiar, but putting them into practice evidently remains elusive. Here's what they said:

- **Lesson One: Avoid the pitfall of assuming more money is the only way to achieve greater quality.**

It is tempting to improve a program by adding more people or by spending more money. Unfortunately, throwing money at a program does not always make it better, but it always makes it bigger and, therefore, harder to pay for. Sometimes quality can be improved by taking money or people from the weaker programs and putting them into the stronger programs.

Reviewing what you do and how you do it, re-engineering processes, and zero-basing departmental budgets are legitimate ways to improve quality. Sometimes the benefits are more reliable and sustainable than what you could get just by spending more money.

- **Lesson Two: Budgeting is about making choices and setting priorities.**

A budget is an investment of resources: Pick the right investments to achieve your goals. Too often budgeting begins and ends with forcing revenue to equal expenditures.

Try this exercise: Write down the strategy and priorities you believe are guiding your nonprofit's future. Now, take your nonprofit's budget and write down the strategy and priorities suggested by how money is spent. Most times you will find they don't match very well.

Make sure strategy and priorities are specifically identified in the budget. How resources are allocated in each year's budget is as central to the strategic plan as the annual board retreat.

- **Lesson Three: Be sure you anticipate what effects your budget will have on staff behavior.**

For every budget rule you create, a behavior or a relationship will be changed. Consider, for instance, two common rules in public-sector budgeting: The budget is specified at the line item rather than by broad category – that rule shifts discretion from the executive to the legislature. Money must be used by the end of the year – that rule gives departments an incentive to spend every dime by the end of the year, even if the money goes to low-priority items.

Make sure your budget rules prompt behaviors that match your priorities.

- **Lesson Four: Development and maintenance of human resources is as necessary as development and maintenance of buildings and equipment.**

Most nonprofits are service organizations, yet while they will have capital campaigns for buildings, they rarely have fundraising campaigns for people skills, and they too often have insignificant programs to train or retain staff.

No organization is static; people come and go; program needs evolve. Good budgets provide resources to replace the skills lost due to staff turnover and to build the new skills required by change.

Many nonprofit boards have building committees that do engineering reviews of physical facilities; how many boards have anything more than a compensation committee for their "human facilities?"

- **Lesson Five: Decisions to invest in bricks and mortar should focus most heavily on what happens after the ribbon is cut.**

Over time, the costs of operating a building and of running the programs in the building are vastly higher than the construction cost. Too often new facilities have turned a fiscally sound institution into one that is continually strapped for cash.

The ability to raise funds for a new building is the least of your financial worries. After your donors have reached deep into their pockets for your capital campaign, they may have less available for your annual campaign. Ironically, now your annual campaign will probably ask for more. Go back to Lesson One.

These lessons are what the best finance officers want to teach over and over again. You could do worse than to put this lesson plan on your organization's agenda.

■ Profit versus Passion

Most people refer to tax-exempt organizations as non-profits. That unfortunate term is misinterpreted too often as a license to lose money, commonly expressed as "Of course they lose money, they're a nonprofit."

It is doubly unfortunate because it is wrong-headed: Nonprofits need profits to survive, just like any other business. What separates tax-exempt organizations from taxable organizations is not whether they earn a profit, but how they spend their profit. If a nonprofit always loses money, it will fail, no differently than any company will fail.

A nonprofit providing some profitable services is not bad or greedy or dishonest; it is doing what is necessary. In exchange for granting tax-exemption, however, society does impose limits.

Most importantly, a nonprofit must use its profit to support the level, quality, or reliability of its services. It doesn't use its profit to pay dividends to supporters, to award out-sized salaries or bonuses to its staff or board, nor to finance expensive office facilities or travel and entertainment that cannot be clearly connected and justified with respect to service delivery.

There are many reasons why nonprofits need profits. Oftentimes, for example, the services that nonprofits provide are most needed or hardest to finance during economic recessions. The only way to weather bad economic times is to set aside some money in good times. The only way to get money to set aside is to earn more money than you spend; that is a profit.

Most nonprofits provide a number of different services that vary in their capacity to pay for themselves. A viable nonprofit usually makes its ends meet by offering some services that do not fully pay for themselves (unprofitable services) and some services that bring in more money than they cost (profitable services).

While commercial businesses may have some items or services that they sell at a loss (loss-leaders), the role of loss-leaders is to attract customers that will simultaneously purchase profitable items so that the total purchases of that customer are profitable.

In contrast, a nonprofit is willing to have all the purchases of some customers be unprofitable. For example, nonprofit hospitals usually lose money in their emergency rooms as well as on uninsured patients. They usually remain financially viable by making money in their cardiac and orthopedic wards (which is one reason why they are so concerned about for-profit specialty hospitals).

Similarly, museums often lose money on school groups but make money on gift shops.

A mix of profitable and unprofitable activities is desirable because it allows the nonprofit the most flexibility in fulfilling its mission and benefiting its community.

Nonprofits that take the extreme position that all their services should be unprofitable are jeopardizing their future ability to provide any services. At the opposite extreme, nonprofits that do not offer any unprofitable services may be shortchanging their mission and missing important opportunities to benefit their community.

Which is better for the community – providing in-home meals only to elderly residents who can pay the cost, or providing a mix of meals at a loss to indigent elderly offset by meals at a modest profit to elderly who can afford to pay? Which is a more valuable mission – charging a uniform entrance fee to all visitors or running a loss from lower prices for students which is balanced by running a profit from gift shop sales to students who can afford such purchases? A mix that includes both profitable and unprofitable services will likely provide the greater benefit to the community.

The conscious decision to earn profits and the choice and mix of profitable and unprofitable activities can determine whether a nonprofit fulfills and sustains its mission or falls short and fails.

Next time you hear someone say, "Of course they lose money, they're a nonprofit," give them a piece of your mind.

■ The Business of Nonprofits

Recently, I spent time talking with successful nonprofit leaders about the issues that most challenge them. One that regularly crops up is the internal tension created by being businesslike in a nonprofit.

An approach to nonprofit management that seems obvious to the for-profit sector may be interpreted by a nonprofit's most passionate supporters as a betrayal of mission in favor of profit. This tension reflects a gap in understanding of what it means for a nonprofit to be businesslike.

This gap is not bridged by introducing business jargon or the latest fad from the business management bookshelf. Instead, bridge this gap by helping your staff, board, and donors to understand that successful fulfillment of mission requires disciplined action in these seven areas:

• Overcome the fear of growing up

Ruth McCambridge, the editor of *Nonprofit Quarterly*, noted in a recent e-newsletter that every nonprofit must face the painful transition from organizational adolescence to maturity.

"Informality that is the energy and soul of a young organization … is a very positive force at first, but eventually you have to either grow out of it or the organization remains dangerously adolescent – and in and out of trouble over its lifetime," she wrote.

For-profit organizations face a similar challenge and most fail to make the transition as evidenced by the high failure rate among small businesses.

The key to successful maturity in a nonprofit is to recognize the need for more structure and formality while preserving passion for the mission. Every successful non-profit executive that I have talked with has found repeated face-to-face communication with board, staff and volunteers is essential to build the necessary confidence and trust that the movement toward formality also comes with a disciplined passion and commitment to the mission.

• **Manage your human resources**

As an organization becomes larger, structure needs to replace intuition. Hiring needs to include reference checks and background checks. Departures need to include meaningful exit interviews. Continual professional development for all staff needs to be as essential and routine as building maintenance.

• **Base all decision-making on a viable strategy**

At all times a successful business knows where it is going. There should be a strategy for how you plan to fulfill your mission, and it should be a meaningful guide for all major financial and operational decisions.

There should be strategic planning at least every three years that involves your board, staff, donors, patrons, and clients. Staff should develop goals and objectives afresh for each new year. Your annual budget should be built around strategy, goals, and objectives so that you can demonstrate that your budget links mission to money.

• **Be objective and realistic about resources**

A mature organization knows that, no matter how committed are its supporters, it alone is responsible for its success and survival. That responsibility means you know what resources you have available, you do the best you can with those resources, and you don't overextend yourself.

Without losing the passion to meet the need, a successful organization must be objective about what it can sustain. Even in the for-profit sector, growth based on unrealistic assumptions of revenue is a primary cause of failure.

• Replace instinct with measurement

A young organization can often thrive on seat-of-the-pants efforts and instinct, but a mature one has a size or complexity that makes that approach misleading and dangerous. While community need was obvious early on, you need to develop empirical measures of the community needs your mission is addressing: Who are you trying to help? What are their needs? How has the "who" or the "what" changed in the past year? You also need to be able to measure what you are doing and its impact.

As you grow, you must be able to know bang for the buck for each of your activities if you are to manage your priorities and maintain your overall effectiveness.

• View the board as a catalyst for success

As a nonprofit grows and staff take on tasks that were once performed by board members, there is a tendency for the board to become an oversight or fundraising body and for board meetings to be viewed as a necessary evil and a burden on staff.

A successful nonprofit chooses each board member for a specific skill and each board member has a purposeful task to perform between each board meeting. In successful nonprofits, board meetings are decision-focused and board members fill skill gaps that staff cannot fill.

• Regularly reinvest in your administrative infrastructure

A serious business develops its management, uses up-to-date information technology, and devotes resources to improving its measurement capabilities. Unfortunately, there can be a perverse nonprofit pride in being tattered as a demonstration of commitment to mission, often unwittingly encouraged by donors who restrict their gifts to programs only or who favor nonprofits with unreasonably low administrative expenses.

A mature, businesslike nonprofit must be unyielding in its insistence that adequate resources be invested in its administrative infrastructure.

Businesslike organizations – for-profit and nonprofit alike – are disciplined and focused in these seven areas. A nonprofit with this discipline has the best of both worlds: It is businesslike with passion.

■ Cash Reserves, Part I

While endowment often gets the most attention in the nonprofit world, it would be better to shift the spotlight to cash reserves. I attribute this lack of attention to hopelessness and confusion.

Hopelessness comes from the tension a nonprofit manager faces between managing for stability and being responsive to donor and constituent pressures to expand. The passion and community need that form the backbone of the nonprofit sector create a relentless pressure to always do more. And the more recent emphasis in the donor community on restricted grants, seed funding and other tools of the "effective philanthropy" movement also adds to the pressure to do more.

Stable management requires financial resiliency, which is provided by having sufficient cash to weather temporary crises. Managers who would want to ask donors to contribute to cash reserves or to ask constituents to be patient so operating surpluses can accumulate cash can be forgiven if they conclude this is a hopeless quest.

Confusion comes from the utter inadequacy of nonprofit accounting in making it easy to assess a nonprofit's need for cash. One of my most popular workshops helps the lay reader to interpret nonprofit financial statements. In that workshop we show a balance sheet that would be considered healthy if it were a for-profit company but which indicates near-insolvency for the nonprofit it represents.

The reasons for this confusion are the numerous restrictions nonprofits face on how its money can be used.

If a for-profit business has a lot of cash and securities on its balance sheet, or if its current assets far exceed its current liabilities, one can be pretty sure the company could weather a sizable storm.

One can't be so certain when it comes to nonprofits. Cash can be completely unavailable for operations if it is held in an endowment, or it can be unavailable to help in a crisis if it is part of a grant that restricts it to uses unrelated to the crisis. Only that part of reported cash that isn't subject to any limitations is comparable to cash on a for-profit's balance sheet. The same warning applies to securities and to current assets. In fact, it is quite possible for a nonprofit with large cash balances and net current assets to have insufficient resources available to pay its bills or weather a crisis.

When cash truly is king

Cash and liquidity can get adequate attention from executives, boards, and donors only if hopelessness and confusion can be overcome. One way to start is to clearly and simply define:

- What assets do we consider for inclusion in the cash reserve that contributes to stability in a nonprofit?

- How should we define the need for cash reserves?

- How large a cash reserve is enough?

The answer to the first question is straightforward: Only the cash and securities that can be made available for any purpose within one to two days should be considered part of the cash reserve. Immediately available, unrestricted cash is likely to be substantially less than the amount shown as cash or current assets in the nonprofit's financial statements.

The definition of cash need must take into account that large corporations have different needs than small businesses; similarly firms with large seasonal fluctuations have different needs than companies with steadier environments.

The most basic definition must address the routine challenges of any seasonal business. Identify the months with the lowest revenue and sum up the amount they fall short of expenses in those months. Then look at the lowest two revenue months you have had in the past several years and add the shortfall in those two months to the sum. This is the minimum amount of cash you should have at all times just to sustain your operations through normal fluctuations.

But the minimum is not enough because surprises happen. Boilers break, roofs fail, computers crash, pledges come in late, and overtime or temporary workers must be paid. To deal with surprises, establish a bank line of credit sufficient to deal with unanticipated repairs of systems or equipment that are critical to maintaining daily operations. If that isn't possible, the nonprofit's cash reserve must also be able to support the largest one or two surprises. Having working capital reserves equal to 5 percent of expenditures is commonly recommended.

Rather than rely on rules of thumb, managers should evaluate the types of risks they face and establish target reserves accordingly. I suggest a cash reserve large enough to deal with normal seasonal revenue fluctuations and the possibility of a one- to two-month delay in receipt of the major donations or grants that are included in your budget.

Being reliable and stable is perhaps more important to fulfilling a nonprofit organization's mission than growing and adding programs.

Remind donors that, with regard to cash reserves, lean can sometimes be too mean – for your mission and for the people who rely on your nonprofit being there when they need you most.

■ Cash Reserves, Part II

Adequate cash is fundamental to the smooth functioning, even survival, of an organization. A chronic shortage of cash is a signal you need to change how you raise funds, how you budget, or how you fundamentally approach balancing growth with sustainability.

A board needs to know at all times if there is enough cash in the organization's checkbook to pay its bills in full and on time for the remainder of the year. It should also know when any extraordinary steps are taken to make the end-of-year checkbook look better than it was at other times during the year.

I recommend board meetings routinely discuss and review three key questions:

- **How much cash are we supposed to have? Do we have policies on holding sufficient cash?**

There is no magic amount of cash that is appropriate for an organization or that will guarantee the wolf stays away from the door. However, the board should identify the minimum cash required for operations to continue uninterrupted.

This means preparing and discussing a monthly forecast of cash inflows and outflows and identifying the months that are likely to be the most challenging. It also means establishing ahead of time a Plan B to implement if cash balances fall below that minimum.

Sufficient cash also means the board needs to know its policies on contingency, working capital, and board-designated reserves. It needs to assure that those policies are being adhered to at all times and that real cash, not pledges or receivables, is filling those reserve buckets.

The board should know the sources of the cash. An adept controller will juggle cash from restricted reserves or endowments in order to meet short-term operating cash requirements. The board should know about this and make sure there are reliable plans to repay that cash promptly and completely.

- **Is there anything in the coming year that could have a significant impact on our cash?**

It is especially important that the board spend as much time looking at major future cash events as it spends looking at the current cash situation. Arts organizations often have major productions that require significant cash outlays. Does the cash-flow forecast identify the months those large outlays are likely to occur and does the forecast provide strong reassurance that sufficient cash will be available in those months?

The board needs to use the cash forecast to evaluate its risks if something goes wrong. Is the organization counting on receiving some major grants or major pledges? If the grant is denied or the pledge delayed in payment, have you identified special actions that can ensure sufficient cash to meet normal operations?

The board should also know where its cash is kept. Is there an investment policy and is the cash invested in ways that are consistent with the likely need to draw on that cash? Is the policy being followed?

- **How did we achieve the level of cash that we show at the end of the fiscal year?**

A responsible board needs to look back at least once a year to summarize and review how staff managed cash flow during the year. This is especially important at year-end, when the snapshot provided by audited financial statements can paint a cash picture that is not representative of situations earlier in the year.

The board should know what was the longest time during the year the organization held off paying bills or borrowed cash to pay bills, and what amounts were involved. Were there any special efforts or events that allowed the organization to catch up on bills or repay any large borrowings?

It is particularly important for boards to know how much of that end-of-year cash balance came from prepayments, memberships, or subscriptions because the expenses that match these inflows will be demanding cash in the coming months.

The virtue of nonprofits is that they do so much with so little. The downside is that they can be particularly vulnerable to bad luck if the management and board are not obsessively vigilant in watching how cash will flow in and out during the year.

Add these questions to the beginning of every board meeting so that they become a routine part of every meeting. Your vigilance with cash is the best way you can protect the sustainability of your mission.

■ Multiyear Financial Planning

Multiyear financial planning is an invaluable tool to maintain a tight linkage between a nonprofit's mission and the shifting needs of the community. Unfortunately, too few organizations use this tool because they wrongly characterize it as an error-prone and futile effort to predict the future.

This mischaracterization is understandable. Everyday we see weather forecasts for rain that never arrives, Wall Street forecasts of earnings that never materialize, and announcements of new products that never get manufactured.

The value of a long-term plan does not lie in its forecasting prowess. Rather, its value comes from providing a way to systematically and consistently:

- Consider future scenarios confronting the organization and the community.

- Examine the consequences of each scenario.

- Illustrate the cumulative effects of key decisions.

- Determine the best responses to prepare for the opportunities and the risks that appear most critical in the coming years.

Limitations of Forecasts

Let's first set some realistic expectations. An intelligent forecast does not build its credibility on being right about what will happen. If accurate prediction of the future were a prerequisite for planning, none of us would compile to-do lists or pick the best time for a summer vacation.

The obvious reason we plan is to identify what events need to occur and in what order so that we can prepare for an outcome we want. The reasons for planning in an organization are not so different.

The most important definition of a good forecast is that it tells a story or suggests a future that makes sense and is consistent with all the other information you have available.

I spent many years building statistical forecasting models and I learned that neither data nor statistics should ever override common sense, judgment, or experience. The most basic test of a forecast is not its complexity or sophistication, but whether it passes this smell test: does it make sense, does it inform policy-making, and do its implications fit with what you know?

Left Behind

One of the keys to staying relevant as a nonprofit organization is to stay in touch with the changing needs of the community. Remember that tax-exemption was created to encourage organizations to address important needs of the community that the for-profit, market-driven economy couldn't or wouldn't address. That critical link between community need and mission cannot be taken for granted; community needs are continually changing and nonprofits must keep up with those changes if they are to remain pertinent.

A multiyear plan starts by examining the major drivers of change in the community. This effort leads to a strategic view of where the community is headed.

Surely, a well-managed nonprofit already has a clear idea of how its programs address the needs of the community. It is a simple step then to ask how well its programs will continue to address community need if things change.

It is highly likely that asking this question will prompt ideas for ways in which the nonprofit could respond. These ideas are the beginning of a multiyear plan.

Next the planning process takes each idea and addresses these questions:

- How does it advance the nonprofit's priorities?

- What outcome is expected and how will it be measured?

- How is the outcome to be reached, when and by whom?

- How will the community benefit after implementation?

Only after an idea survives the gauntlet of these questions does the planning process get into the financial issues of personnel, costs, revenue, and overall affordability. These, in turn, raise other important questions:

- Do we change the business model?

- Do we change our approach to fundraising?

- Do we change our cost structure?

- Should we grow, shrink, merge?

The result of these efforts is a multiyear plan that represents the best thinking about what the nonprofit needs to do next. The budget is the first step in that plan.

Oh yes, a forecast played a part in answering all these questions. But it wasn't the forecast that was important; rather, its role was as a tool to ensure the strategic Q&A was internally consistent and incorporated the implications of each option.

The only way to keep up with change is to have a process to evaluate it and develop responsive strategies.

No one has yet discovered a better tool for this than multiyear planning. It helps you keep your eye on the strategic ball amid the noise and distractions of daily operations.

■ Community Needs

The most effective budgets are seen as plans of action that result from a clear set of goals intended to advance the nonprofit's mission to serve a community need.

While this approach to budgeting may seem abstract, it is actually quite similar to what for-profits do routinely. Most of us are familiar with the following phrases describing the reality to which for-profit businesses continually adapt: follow the market, keep up with changing demand, identify consumer preferences.

The reality to which an effective nonprofit must continually adapt is similar, although the phrases are different: know the changes in your community, keep up with community need, and stay relevant.

As part of budget preparation, you should reassess the links between your current services, mission, and the community need they are intended to address. While sometimes this is part of a major strategic planning exercise, every year should include some effort to re-examine its relevance and effectiveness.

What's the Need?

While a for-profit business is accustomed to adapting to changing consumer demands, nonprofits too often get trapped into preserving a mission that serves an outdated community need. It is a mistake to assume that community needs don't change over time. It is also a mistake to presume that yesterday's mission must be tomorrow's mission.

Be open-minded as you reassess community need and how your mission can adapt to current need. Sometimes reassessment indicates tweaking your mission and your services; sometimes it indicates your mission may no longer be important or your impact on the mission may no longer be effective.

When you see the latter situation emerging, you should look at other organizations nearby that address similar missions to see if they are in similar straits. If they seem to be doing better, there may be continued community demand for and support for the mission. If so, it may be most effective to consider merging with them or redirecting your resources to match their more current definition and delivery of mission.

The United Way of America is a timely example of a nonprofit that believes there has been a major change in community need and has made substantial changes in its mission as a result. In changing its mission, it redefined its role from being passively supportive of the nonprofits' approach to addressing community needs to a role of determining community needs and influencing how and which nonprofits can best meet those demands.

The key to this decision was an assessment that community demands had changed from the need for streamlined fundraising to the need for proof that donated money is used effectively. To its credit, the United Way adjusted its mission to match its new assessment.

Still, some may be skeptical that this is an appropriate change. But the skepticism should be based on the accuracy of the assessment of community need, not on whether it is appropriate to change mission.

In order to remain relevant a nonprofit must regularly assess the community need it seeks to serve.

Changing with the times brings the risk of misreading the times. And major changes bring greater risks.

United Way's determination to be responsive is taking a risk. There is no guarantee its changes will be successful, and there is no guarantee it has made a correct reading of community need.

Back to the Budget

Regardless of the potential for risk, community need is the reality that should guide strategic decisions. And the budget should represent the next step in carrying out that strategy.

As community needs change, the nonprofit should change. Most often this is tweaking and sometimes it is dramatic.

While risk must always be weighed against the anticipated benefits of the change, it is important to remember that the status quo also brings its own risks – the risks of irrelevance, ineffectiveness, or possibly failure.

What is important is continual vigilance to stay relevant to the needs of the community and the courage to insist that community need be linked to mission, mission to action, and action to accomplishment.

As you start to prepare next year's budget, reassess the strength of these three linkages and identify a plan of action and change that best ties your accomplishments to the current needs of the community.

■ Endowment, Part I

Nonprofits are caught in the crossfire of a weak economy and rising costs. This has created budget pressures that some think can be relieved by building an endowment.

At the extreme, endowment is held out as a silver bullet that will ensure the financial stability of a nonprofit. This is a dangerous misconception. If not approached carefully, shifting fundraising efforts toward accumulation of endowment has the potential to seriously weaken and destabilize a nonprofit.

An endowment is a concept that is unique to nonprofits and foundations. Endowment is a sizable pool of money that is set aside in perpetuity. Only the investment income from the endowment, but never the original principal, is intended to support the operations of the nonprofit. The idea is for a nonprofit to save for the future by making part of its assets unavailable today, regardless of current need.

But this unavailability, and its consequences on current financial health, place nonprofits in stark contrast to for-profit businesses, which have complete access to all their assets to grow and support operations in good times and in bad.

Prior to considering shifting fundraising efforts toward building an endowment, it is important that nonprofit executives and trustees understand these facts:

- Endowment practice requires the future be provided for before the present. It is a misconception to believe newly raised endowment will be a source of near-term operating support.

The underlying principle of modern endowment management is that the primary fiduciary responsibility of the board of trustees is to preserve the future buying power of every endowment gift.

This obligation means that the first dollar of investment income must be reinvested to cover future anticipated inflation so that the inflation-adjusted buying power of the endowment principal is never reduced. Only after this future inflation is financed can one take money out to support current operations. As a result, endowments must grow before one can use any money to support current services.

- One can guarantee to future generations stable annual endowment spending or a stable value of the endowment, but not both. It is a misconception to believe both goals can be achieved – and stable spending is usually the loser.

Overall, when endowments plunge along with the stock market, endowment spending is reduced. Even nonprofits with sizable endowments make this choice, a result of the tension between operating needs and fiduciary obligations.

In a poor investment year, for example, one cannot spend and reinvest the same amounts as in the previous year. If one is to remain at the same amount, the other must decrease.

Though the nonprofit's operating staff wants inflation-adjusted spending to remain the same, the board, as trustees of the endowment, prefer the inflation-adjusted value of the endowment to stay the same. It is no surprise therefore that, when the stock market plunges, many nonprofits' spending rates are reduced to preserve the endowment's value, weakening rather than stabilizing the nonprofit's current operations.

- Raising endowment shifts resources from the present to the future. Can your organization afford this shift?

The decision to raise an endowment is a decision to focus some current fundraising on building a nest egg – albeit a very restricted one – that is highly unlikely to support or stabilize service delivery in the next five years. The previous points have already made it clear that the impact of the year-to-year volatility of the investment markets falls most harshly on current operations.

This greater exposure to investment volatility, combined with a shift of resources toward the future, creates a potential vulnerability that a nonprofit must carefully consider.

It's true that it is easier to set aside a nest egg for the future if you are wealthy than if you are poor. A nonprofit must first ask itself, therefore, whether its financial health for the next five years is secure enough to be able to shift some of today's resources toward providing for service delivery 50 years from now. Nonprofits that are blessed with strong support from an endowment are benefiting from a choice made decades ago – and are lucky that choice did not fatally destabilize them in the intervening years.

Your primary obligation as a nonprofit manager is to be a reliable provider of a service that fulfills a useful need in the community. Because of this, your first duty is to ensure your reliability for the next five years before you begin to worry about being reliable 50 years from now.

Do you have sufficient current revenue to produce operating surpluses or repay your debt? Do you have sufficient cash reserves to stabilize your spending from year to year?

Do you have money set aside for predictable major replacement expenses, such as computers, roofs, vehicles, and building systems?

Only if you have answered yes to all three questions may raising an endowment be the right next step in your financial plan.

■ Endowment, Part II

One of my most spirited workshops discusses the uses and abuses of endowments in sustaining a nonprofit's mission. It is easy to be seduced by the potential benefits of endowment: It provides a supplement to current income and it can contribute to greater stability in a nonprofit's overall financial health.

Unfortunately, I find too many nonprofit trustees and executives approach endowment as a goal rather than as a tool that must be used carefully and knowledgeably. Tools can be misused and be a cause of volatility rather than sustainability in a nonprofit's mission.

Colleges and universities are prime examples of endowments causing volatility. One survey of university endowments found that as of June 2009, traditional investments in stocks and bonds comprised less than half of endowment assets in favor of alternative strategies such as private equity, venture capital, and hedge funds. Moreover, many, including Harvard, Dartmouth, and Cornell, used endowment income to support one-fourth to almost two-fifths of their operating budgets.

In part due to these two factors, when the markets declined in 2008-2009, volatility followed and universities faced almost 20 percent declines in the value of their endowments and sizable declines in the income distributed to operations. One survey found the disruption to operations to be sizable: over half of the universities surveyed had partial hiring freezes, postponed or cancelled building projects, and made midyear cuts in non-personnel budgets. Over one-third froze or delayed salary increases.

Borrowers beware

In 2006 the Milwaukee Public Museum got into trouble by "borrowing" money from its endowment to sustain spending and cover operating deficits. This practice led to four felony indictments against the museum's chief financial officer, even though the criminal complaint notes "he did not profit personally from his actions." By the way, half the museum staff lost their jobs and two-thirds of the board members were replaced.

Far from horror stories, these examples reflect two, albeit extreme, approaches to the dilemmas of how to invest and spend endowments. No one wants to be labeled a rube for failing to follow high-flying stock markets or hedge funds. And few have the courage to cut operating expenditures when budgets are tight and everyone can see the endowment just sitting there. Rather, everyone hopes financial crises are short-lived so temporary "borrowing" from the endowment seems prudent.

Verne Sedlacek, my former colleague at Harvard Management Company and now CEO at Commonfund, wrote a thoughtful essay on the dilemmas of how to invest and spend from endowments. He reminds us there are three goals that guide modern endowment management:

- Maintaining intergenerational equity by assuring the inflation-adjusted value of the endowment does not decrease.

- Maintaining real spending power in the short term by adjusting spending rates (the percent of endowment withdrawn each year to support operations) for annual inflation.

- Maintaining stability year to year in the level of endowment spending.

No one has yet figured out how to achieve all three. The last two goals usually lose out to the intergenerational goal.

Sedlacek offers three ways to reduce this conflict.

First is asset allocation. This familiar tool requires little discussion. Identifying a mix of assets that provides adequate growth within a tolerable range of year-to-year volatility can support all three goals.

Interestingly, extensive simulation work at Commonfund suggests most nonprofits have at best a 50-50 chance of maintaining intergenerational equity using the common mixes of stocks and bonds and the conventional 5 percent annual withdrawal of endowment to support operations.

Different approaches

Second and most surprising is the continuing need for annual fundraising for the endowment. Sedlacek notes "gifts are a highly positive factor that increase the likelihood of achieving intergenerational equity, enable a nonprofit to spend more for present operations, and reduce the volatility of spending." He goes on to report Commonfund research has found "one-half the dollar increase in the average market value of endowment funds came from gifts and one-half from retained investment return."

He quickly notes the gifts must be current and unrestricted; restricted and deferred gifts do not deliver the same benefit. This finding is ironic and runs counter to much of the current emphasis in philanthropy on restricted and deferred giving.

Furthermore, it highlights that once a nonprofit diverts some of its annual fundraising toward endowment, it must continue to do so in perpetuity if it is to address the three goals above.

Third, Sedlacek finds the conventional three-year moving average approach to calculating the annual withdrawal from the endowment is an inferior way to achieve our three goals. He advocates two other approaches, which he calls banded inflation and hybrid spending.

Banded inflation increases the annual dollar amount withdrawn from the endowment by the rate of annual inflation; however, in no case can the withdrawal go above or below a specific percentage (or band) of the endowment's value.

The hybrid method combines annual inflation and annual investment return by calculating the annual increase or decrease in endowment withdrawal as 0.7 times the inflation rate and 0.3 times the change in the value of the endowment.

Getting stability and sustainability from an endowment is complicated and hard to achieve. A superficial approach to raising and managing an endowment can make the three goals of endowment elusive and mislead trustees that the endowment is supporting the nonprofit as a reliable provider to an important community need.

If your nonprofit is ready to consider raising an endowment, start doing your homework now.

■ Investments, Part I

Recently I attended a finance committee meeting of one of my nonprofit clients and we were debating whether to go ahead with a project that would require about six years for the nonprofit to recover its money. At this point, a new board member with extensive financial expertise in the for-profit sector said:

"That's a 17 percent return, and in my business we would jump at the opportunity."

Hearing that, I knew it was time to write about the paradox of nonprofit capital investment and how decision-making based on return on investment can starve a nonprofit's highest mission-related activities.

Nonprofit capital scarce

A critical factor in evaluating an investment is how much an organization must invest of its own money.

Most nonprofits hold the bulk of their nonphysical assets in restricted form, which means management has no discretion in how the money is used. As a result, the few assets that are under management's control are particularly valuable as a cushion for operations.

In other words, an unrestricted dollar today is more valuable than a future dollar resulting from an investment. This reality sets a high bar – technically a high discount rate or internal rate of return – for a potential investment to overcome.

This bar is much higher than most for-profit companies would set for their investments. Moreover, a for-profit business can seek bank financing. Unfortunately for most nonprofits, a lack of unrestricted assets often renders them unqualified for bank financing.

Most nonprofits have capital fundraising campaigns and wait until the money is raised before investing in their business. This approach means nonprofit capital projects need to have much higher unleveraged rates of return. It is rare to have a capital campaign more than once every five years. Imagine a for-profit company trying to thrive if it were hamstrung with either limitation in its investment program.

High returns, low on mission

Limiting investments to only grand slams may not seem so bad. Unfortunately, high returns collide with the nonprofit's goal to place emphasis on providing services that cannot be provided by the for-profit sector.

The label "nonprofit" is literally true for the highest mission activities. Investment in high mission will not create profit and will not show compelling returns.

On the other hand, nonprofits have low-mission activities precisely so they can earn profit that can be used to support unprofitable, high-mission activities.

Let's reconsider that board member's suggestion that 17 percent is a good standard for worthwhile investments. This return is higher than any high-mission investment can produce. At the same time, because nonprofit capital is so scarce, it is far too low a return to demand from low-mission activities, which justify diverting capital away from high-mission activities only when they are highly profitable.

So perhaps 17 percent is not the right number. If the project is being done to earn a profit, maybe that scarce capital should require a 33 percent return so the investment dollars can be recaptured quickly to use for higher-mission needs. A 33 percent return is likely possible only if the nonprofit puts a very small amount of its own capital into the project and seeks outside donors or lenders, who will likely insist on profit-making investments.

Investment paradox

Nonprofits have an incentive to seek outside funding for investments in the lowest-mission activities where they can better leverage their scarce capital. Similarly, outside funders want the greatest return for their investments or donations, which is most easily found in low-mission, but profitable activities.

And there lies the paradox: The most important areas to invest in are elsewhere: the low-return, high mission activities.

We need a new approach to measuring the value of nonprofit investments. It needs to solve the paradox that conventional financial measures steer outside capital away from high mission investments. If we don't, then we will be pushing our nonprofits away from mission and into the for-profit world.

■ Investments, Part II

There has been a great deal of attention paid to banking problems and losses. Many nonprofits are concerned about where they should be placing their money.

The answers will vary depending on when that money will be needed and for what purpose. In general, the so-called investment market should be limited to funds that are not needed for more than two to three years and for which there is a tolerance for temporary loss of principal in exchange for a likelihood of higher income over a period of five years or more. Uses for these monies is a very short list: endowments, reserves for major facility repairs, and reserves you will not need to draw upon in two to three years.

All other funds should be placed in short-term investments with little or no risk to principal. There are basically five short-term investments nonprofits should consider.

Bank checking deposits should be held by every nonprofit. These deposits are immediately available, pay little or no interest, and are insured by the Federal Deposit Insurance Corporation (FDIC) up to certain limits.

Bank certificates of deposit (CDs) pay interest for a specified period of time, often ranging from one month to several years. In general, these funds cannot be accessed before the maturity of the CD without significant penalties. The principal is insured by the FDIC up to certain limits. Multiple CDs can be assembled with sequential maturities so that funds can become available weekly, monthly, or quarterly.

Money market deposit accounts (MMDAs and not to be confused with money market mutual funds MMMFs) are bank deposits that are immediately available subject to monthly limits on the number of withdrawals and pay interest that can vary. The principal is insured by the FDIC up to certain limits.

To determine the extent of insurance coverage for a nonprofit's total bank deposits, go to http://www.fdic.gov/edie for an estimator of coverage. A nonprofit can expand its insurance coverage by holding deposits in more than one bank. This is most practical for CDs, which can be acquired from multiple banks directly through a brokerage house. Just be sure to have in writing the name of each bank issuing each CD, the exact date of maturity of each CD, the method of interest calculation, and proof of FDIC insurance coverage for each bank.

Treasury bills are Federal government securities that have maturities ranging from four weeks to 52 weeks. The majority of Treasury bills issued mature in 13 weeks, often called 90-day T-bills. They are sold at a discount from the face value paid to the holder at maturity.

There is no market risk to principal if the security is held to maturity. T-bills can be purchased directly from the Treasury or from a broker. They can be sold prior to maturity only if purchased through a broker but the market value will vary from the face value. Like bank CDs, T-bills can be assembled with sequential maturities.

Money market mutual funds are mutual funds sold by brokerage houses. The brokerage house promises but does not guarantee that balances are immediately available and that principal will be protected. Historically these promises were firm; however, in the market turmoil of 2008 several money market mutual funds failed to make funds available or to protect principal. These accounts do not have FDIC insurance.

These five short-term investment vehicles are appropriate for certain purposes:

For immediate needs bank checking accounts and money market deposit accounts are most appropriate.

Reserves against accounts receivable should be held only in bank checking accounts and money market deposit accounts. If a nonprofit typically has grants or contracts that pay by reimbursement, it needs working capital to cover its expenses while waiting for reimbursement. Some nonprofits see delays of three to five months after the expenses are incurred. Since the nonprofit is essentially a lender to the grantor, it needs to have sufficient deposits to cover this implicit loan, and these funds need to be risk free and immediately available.

Escrowed funds can be appropriately held in bank checking accounts, money market deposit accounts, and CDs. Escrowed funds, such as tuition or subscription receipts, are monies that would have to be paid back if performances didn't occur or enrollment was cancelled. These funds need to be free of principal risk but the time line is more certain so that the longer maturities of CDs can be appropriate and may boost income.

Reserves for seasonal fluctuations can be held in bank money market deposit accounts, CDs, or T-bills. Seasonality is fairly predictable so the liquidity of checking accounts is unnecessary and the higher income available from these investments is valuable. Because the size of these reserves is large but expenditure fairly certain, FDIC insurance is essential, ruling out the use of uninsured money market mutual funds.

Reserves for revolving program reinvestments can be held in CDs, T-bills, or money market mutual funds. These reserves set aside funds in one or more years in order to accumulate enough for reinvestments in programs or facilities that are more expensive than could be paid for from one year's revenue, including receipts from capital campaigns. Rainy Day reserves can also be held in CDs, T-bills, or money market mutual funds. The longer holding period for these purposes warrants taking higher liquidity or principal risk in order to earn extra income. However, because of the certainty of spending the funds within a few years, longer-term investments remain inappropriate.

A nonprofit has many needs for holding money that must be safely and reliably available. The investment markets are not appropriate for these funds because the risk exceeds the benefit from higher income.

IV. LEGAL ISSUES

Nonprofits are corporations subject to special federal and state laws and accounting rules that differ from what for-profits face.

Nonprofits have legal privileges that come with statutory and regulatory limitations on their behavior. The term "nonprofits" generally refers to organizations that have qualified for federal tax exemption under the legal restrictions of Section 501(c)(3) of the Internal Revenue Code. Nonprofits are exempt from federal and most state taxation and donations to them are deductible from the gross taxable income of the donor. In return nonprofits are prohibited from involvement in elections of public officials and they are subject to restrictions on their spending to influence legislation. Virtually all nonprofits must file IRS Form 990 annually, which discloses financial information as well as information on programs, officers, board members, and large donors.

Nonprofits also face limitations on their use of capital which for-profits do not face. Endowments are assets which nonprofits can invest and access subject to limitations spelled out in state law and donor gift documentation. In contrast reserves can be accessed quickly and in their entirety. In a difficult economy, wise nonprofits favor accumulating reserves over accumulating endowments.

Nonprofits also face limitations on how they can use gifts. In contrast to for-profit equity investments which can be spent in any way, many donors who invest money in nonprofits limit what the money can be used for. These restrictions complicate knowing the true liquidity and solvency of a nonprofit. It is quite possible to be rich in restricted gifts yet so poor in unrestricted cash that it is difficult to make payroll.

The Sarbanes Oxley Act early in the millennium imposed regulations on for-profits regarding their governance, oversight, risk management, and financial reporting. While nonprofits are not subject to this law, increasingly nonprofits are expected by the IRS and major philanthropies to comply with the spirit of the law. Without the benefit of a single federal law, nonprofits find themselves subject to divergent and sometimes conflicting requirements of multiple donors and governmental grantors.

■ Basic Duties

Every nonprofit has two basic duties: To provide a service that fulfills a useful need in the community, and to sustain that service through good times and bad.

The "useful need" duty is imbedded in U.S. tax law; duty to "sustain" is an acknowledgment that a community thrives best when it can rely on the services its nonprofits provide.

Most people use the term nonprofits to refer to tax-exempt charitable organizations. Technically, they are a 501(c)(3), which refers to the section of the Internal Revenue Code that grants the organization federal tax-exempt status.

That status was granted because the organization and its assets are devoted "exclusively" and "permanently" to fulfilling one of nine community needs ("exempt purposes"), such as relief for the underprivileged, advancement of education, lessening the burdens of government or the tensions in neighborhoods, defense of human rights or combating community deterioration. Whatever the private sector and the government can do in these nine areas, our society has decided it is not enough and must be supplemented by a healthy, vibrant nonprofit sector.

Tax exemption is our society's method to encourage strong financial support of this sector by individuals and corporations.

Answering call in tough times

The services that nonprofits provide, these "exempt purposes," have become so essential in our society that we have come to count on them always being around – homeless shelters, hospitals, health clinics, museums, food pantries, concerts, plays, neighborhood centers, preschools.

Unfortunately, many nonprofits lurch from crisis to crisis. They expand until economic recessions put them in financial crises that force them to cut services, often when the community need is the greatest.

Whether a nonprofit is in the arts, social services, health care or another arena, the need for what it does won't go away when the economy falters. In fact, it is likely the services nonprofits provide are even more central to the vitality of the community when the chips are down. The "exclusive" purpose and "permanent" role cannot be compromised by a focus on getting bigger, expanding services, doing more than last year or becoming the best in the country. The ability of a nonprofit to be there when its services are most needed is referred to as sustainability.

Sustaining the mission of an organization should be the primary task of a nonprofit manager or board member and should form the basis for all important decisions. Steady, reliable and predictable are the right words, but they run up against growth, expansion and "meeting the need."

If you sit on the board of a nonprofit or work for one, when you think about your mission, you should always precede every major decision with the question: How long can we sustain this change or ensure we will be able to provide this service?

The dilemma of sustainability versus growth pervades the nonprofit world. A nonprofit organization has to decide early on how to deal with its ambition to grow and its obligation toward sustainability. Is it better to provide a service and then suspend it when finances are tight? Is it better to not provide the service at all if the service cannot be sustained?

There is no clear cut answer, nor is it always an either-or choice. If a nonprofit grows and later cannot sustain its new level of services, it may jeopardize its survival and hurt the community that relies on its services.

Aiming high, low

But expansion doesn't have to be a dirty word. Rather, expansion should be approached cautiously with a clear, multiyear plan that provides reasonable confidence that the necessary steps have been taken to ensure success and to sustain the new level of services.

The community needs to know that its nonprofits can and will fulfill their roles in the community in fair weather and foul. Choosing the level and breadth of services that are sustainable is a duty that a responsible nonprofit must continually bear in mind.

The Greek myth of Daedalus and Icarus is useful to remember. Needing to escape from the fabled labyrinth, Daedalus fashioned wings of feathers and wax for his son, Icarus, and himself. He warned Icarus to fly neither too low nor too high, for the waves below would soak the feathers and the sun above would melt the wax. Icarus, thrilled with his ability to fly high, ignored the warning and flew so high that the wax melted and he plunged to his death.

Nonprofits face the same balancing act – not to be so cautious that the critical needs of the community remain unmet, nor to aim so high that the organization is endangered and the reliability of its services compromised.

■ Participation in Elections

Passions rise during an election season and well-intentioned nonprofit leaders and trustees can get their organizations into trouble. A nonprofit organization is defined by its mission, which should be passionate and oftentimes emotional. And it is expected that a nonprofit will seek to advance its mission, making involvement in governmental affairs a potential part of that strategy.

There is a sharp distinction, however, between seeking to influence legislation and seeking to influence an election to public office.

It is worthwhile to clarify that we are talking about 501(c)(3) organizations, which are usually referred to as nonprofits. This group includes churches, universities, hospitals, and charitable organizations whose missions fit into a precise definition in the Internal Revenue Code.

There are 32 other types of tax-exempt organizations for whom contributions generally are not tax deductible. The most familiar are business (501(c)(6), labor (501(c)(5), civic (501)(c)(4), and political (527) organizations. They have their own sets of rules.

For 501(c)(3) organizations, lobbying to influence legislation is permitted up to a certain threshold of the nonprofit's activity. In sharp contrast, the IRS makes it clear that nonprofits are "absolutely prohibited from directly or indirectly participating in, or intervening in, any political campaign on behalf of (or in opposition to) any candidate for elective public office." Any violation of this prohibition may result in denial or revocation of tax-exempt status and the imposition of certain excise taxes on the prohibited expenditures.

This prohibition can become confusing in practice, particularly with respect to voter registration, get-out-the-vote efforts, candidate forums, and the personal activities of nonprofit executives and board members. The key determinant is whether the nonprofit activity favors, opposes, or shows any bias toward candidates for public office.

The IRS provides 21 examples of how to interpret this prohibition at http://www.irs.gov/newsroom/article/0,,id=154712,00.html but here we will focus on three areas:

Voter education, registration, and get-out-the-vote efforts: Nonprofits are permitted to encourage people to vote and to aid them in registering to vote. The important factor is that the effort must not emphasize or favor a particular candidate or political party. That means registering a person regardless of the party they choose.

The IRS provides an example in which an environmental organization runs a telephone bank and asks voters about their views on environmental issues. If a voter indicates he favors an environmental candidate for political office, the caller then expands the dialogue to remind the voter of the upcoming election and the importance of voting, ending the call with an offer to provide transportation to the polls. This shift in the conversation violates the prohibition. Before the shift in topic, the call to discuss environmental issues was permissible.

Activity by nonprofit leaders: Nonprofit leaders can have and express opinions regarding candidates for office. This permission requires there be no explicit or implicit association of the person's views with the nonprofit organization.

That means these views cannot be expressed at an official function of the nonprofit, whether it be a board meeting or a public meeting. The view also cannot be expressed in a publication of the organization or using any official material or equipment of the organization.

The safest way for a leader to express such views is in a forum that's not associated with the nonprofit and with a statement that the views are solely his own and do not represent the organization.

Candidate forums and appearances: This area can be the most difficult for an organization. Often nonprofits are logical places for group events and many routinely have speakers and public events in which acknowledging the presence of community leaders is customary.

Acknowledging a public official is permissible if no reference is made by the nonprofit or the official to the individual's candidacy for election. It would be a violation, however, to urge support for the official in gratitude for the official's support of the nonprofit.

Similarly, in advocating issues related to its mission, the nonprofit would be prohibited from including any form of reference that could be associated with a candidate for public office, whether it's a photo or features of a candidate's platform or biography.

All candidates must be invited to an election forum and it must be stated who was invited and who declined the invitation. The topics and questions should not imply any bias for or against any candidate.

Because of the complexity of the law, many nonprofits choose to remain silent during an election campaign. That's unnecessary, but it is vital the organization become familiar with the rules and resources the IRS makes available.

■ Lobbying

The permissibility of lobbying by 501(c)(3) tax-exempt nonprofits is widely misunderstood and many nonprofits needlessly limit their participation in public debates over critical legislation.

Internal Revenue Service regulations permit, and in some ways expect, nonprofits to be engaged in legislative activities as long as it falls within guidelines. Guidelines vary by the type of nonprofit.

The IRS draws a sharp distinction between political and legislative activities. The first is prohibited while the second is not. A nonprofit is "absolutely prohibited from directly or indirectly participating in, or intervening in, any political campaign on behalf of (or in opposition to) any candidate for elective public office."

Moderate Legislative Activity Permitted

In contrast, nonprofits can engage in activities that seek to influence legislation. In fact, since the justification for nonprofit status is to fulfill a community need, influencing legislation that would affect or alleviate the need should often be an essential component of a nonprofit's mission.

Not surprisingly, however, the IRS emphasizes that this activity can be a component of the nonprofit's activities but must not be a "substantial part" of its activities.

The IRS Form 990 Schedule C Part II is the primary test for a nonprofit's lobbying activities. A nonprofit has two ways to demonstrate compliance. The default option is the "substantial part" test consisting of answering yes or no questions and reporting expenditures for lobbying activity.

Under this option, the nonprofit leaves it up to the IRS to determine if this activity is "substantial."

A nonprofit can have a more exact handle on the permissibility of its lobbying activities by choosing to be an "electing public charity" so that the provisions of section 501(h) of the Internal Revenue Code apply. This election requires filing Form 5768 prior to the commencement of a fiscal year.

This "expenditure test" uses a specific test based roughly on the size of lobbying expenditures relative to total spending by the nonprofit. This option may be preferable because the relative size allowed is fairly generous. For example, a nonprofit with $500,000 of mission-related expenditures can spend up to $100,000 on lobbying activities. A nonprofit with mission-related expenditures of $10 million can spend up to $650,000. The largest nonprofits have a lobbying expenditure cap of $1 million a year.

These limits in practice are even more generous because many legislative activities do not count against this cap. For example, communications with a nonprofit's membership regarding legislation of direct interest to its mission do not count against this limit. Nor do expenditures for nonpartisan analysis or research, discussing broad social or economic problems, or appearing before or communicating with any legislative body regarding any legislation affecting the nonprofit organization directly.

Even though these limits seem high, it is imperative nonprofits monitor their compliance. The law sets separate standards for activities to influence the general public and the legislature.

Penalties for exceeding these limits can be severe. Expenditures above these limits are subject to a 25 percent tax on the excess in that year. Excessive lobbying over any four-year period can result in loss of tax-exempt status.

Moreover, there is a possible tax of 5 percent of total lobbying expenditures that can be imposed on an organization's managers, who "agree to including those expenditures knowing the expenditures would likely result in loss of tax-exempt status."

While the regulations can seem complex and the penalties harsh, most nonprofits will find that a focused lobbying program that is coordinated with delivery of its mission is safely within these limits.

Expenditures for monitoring legislation or informing one's membership are virtually unlimited.

At least at the state and local levels, hiring lobbyists to support or oppose particular legislation will almost always remain less than six figures, safely below the limits for any nonprofit with mission-related expenditures of more than $300,000 per year.

And sharing lobbying expenditures with similarly situated nonprofits further reduces the reportable amount.

■ The Sarbanes Oxley Act

In 2002 the Sarbanes Oxley Act, Securities and Exchange Commission, and Public Company Accounting Oversight Board massively increased the amount of reporting and documentation required of publicly-traded companies. As the high cost of compliance has become more apparent, the requirement has been repeatedly delayed or diluted for small companies, and avoided altogether by companies that decided to go private.

Since then, the Internal Revenue Service substantially expanded annual Form 990 reports and expanded public access to Form 990-T reports. The Columbus Foundation rolled out Power Philanthropy, an access and disclosure program based on the Kansas City Community Foundation's DonorEdge program. To this are added reporting programs of the Better Business Bureau's Wise Giving Alliance, the Ohio Association of Nonprofit Organization's Standards of Excellence certification program, the Greater Columbus Arts Council's mandatory reporting for grant recipients, and the United Way's reporting programs and time-consuming advisory committees.

While no one has quantified the cost of complying with so many programs, I suspect that it is equivalent to the cost of at least one full-time employee, or the equivalent of a half-dozen average corporate gifts.

An added irony is that the cost of compliance and reporting adds to the operating expenses of nonprofits at the same time that an increasing number of donors are insisting that their gifts go to programs and not to operating expenses. While for-profit companies do not face spending restrictions from their investors and can avoid the costly reporting of Sarbanes Oxley by going private, nonprofits have no such options.

It is good when the motivation for this increased scrutiny and focus on program giving is to assume a fiduciary duty to justify citizens' trust in the nonprofit. It is not so good when the motivation is to apply a one-size-fits-all measurement of management competence.

John Carver, the corporate governance guru known for his Policy Governance⊠ model, and Jim Collins, the corporate management guru, both provide insights that suggest this explosion of reporting and program giving is missing the mark.

John Carver asked the following question of boards, which also applies to donors: "How can a group of peers be a responsible owner-representative, exercising authority over activities they will never completely see, toward goals they cannot fully measure, through jobs and disciplines they will never master themselves? How can they fulfill their own accountability while not … infringing … on the creativity … of management?"

And Jim Collins applies his *Good to Great* "flywheel" concept to chastise restricted, program giving. "[Program] giving misses a fundamental point: To make the greatest impact on society requires first and foremost a great organization, not a single great program."

In many cases, nonprofits are asked to deal with the community's most intractable problems, and they need to build the capacity to move flexibly and intelligently. Program giving rarely provides this capacity and too often it reduces capacity.

The best motivation for giving is the desire to be part of a successful cause that matters to the community. The explosion in nonprofit reporting and program giving is a sincere but ultimately counterproductive effort to get a handle on success and to identify the nonprofit services that are most effective.

Borrowing Jim Collin's emphasis that success should be defined at the organization level and John Carver's caution that we must separate governance and oversight from management, a sustainable and successful organization needs resources in four key areas: management, governance, unrestricted cash, and staffing.

Here are some productive and effective ways for major donors and especially corporations and foundations to provide resources in a manner that will make them confident that they are supporting a cause that matters and is successful:

Management Resources

Few nonprofits have sufficient resources to buy or to have on staff all the skills needed for a successful organization. Providing a loaned executive for a week, a month, or longer in a specialized area can be enormously helpful.

Skill areas that are often understaffed are project management, facility management, information systems management, interior design and showcasing, market research, and financial analysis.

Ask a nonprofit where it could use some specialized expertise for a project and loan an executive with that expertise.

Governance Resources

Corporations often place one of their staff members on nonprofit boards, but too often that person knows a lot about management but little about governance.

While one motivation for placing staff on boards is akin to major shareholders seeking to protect their investment, membership on a nonprofit board should be motivated by a desire to foster the success of the nonprofit and its chief executive.

For board membership to be an effective resource, it is vital to provide board training to prospective employee-board members lest they bring their management instincts into the boardroom, a sure path to micromanagement or passive attendance, neither of which provides useful resources to a nonprofit.

Financial Resources

The success and sustainability of nonprofits is compromised by the pervasiveness of undercapitalization. Nonprofits need adequate reserve funds and unrestricted cash in order to be viable as much as for-profits need sufficient equity and retained earnings.

Program giving doesn't contribute to unrestricted cash or reserves, and oftentimes it actually drains them by requiring nonprofits to divert resources to lower priority activities in order to meet donor requirements.

Moreover, accumulating reserves requires running surpluses, so that nonprofits with operating surpluses are as much in need of unrestricted financial support as are nonprofits facing deficits.

Staffing Resources

Nonprofits are service providers, which is a labor intensive business.

Providing volunteers for short-term projects or sustained tasks is a wonderful way to supplement the resources of nonprofits and to gain insight into the nonprofit's path to success.

Jim Collins notes that great organizations don't result from a single defining action, grand program, or killer innovation. Rather they result from sustained, persistent efforts "with almost imperceptible progress."

Having a company put its people into the midst of the energy and commitment of a nonprofit is an excellent way to help the organization and to perceive progress and the excitement of being part of something successful.

The definition of success is unique to each nonprofit. As Jim Collins notes, "The confusion between inputs and outputs stems from one of the primary differences between business and [nonprofits]. In business, money is both an input (a resource for achieving greatness) and an output (a measure of greatness).

"In the [nonprofit sector], money is only an input, and not a measure of greatness."

The surge in scrutiny of nonprofits is an effort to apply a one-size-fits-all approach to measuring success at the risk of achieving one-size-fits-none. While reporting can provide benefits, its cost to nonprofits is not trivial and it should not become a shortcut in philanthropic decision-making.

Major donors, foundations, and corporations that are committed to the community should take a broad view of how they provide resources and what they require in return.

Supplementing governance, management, and staffing, as well as providing unrestricted cash, will engage foundations and corporations in ways that can provide the confidence that the resources they is providing are paying off for the community.

And it should reveal the true cost of the burdensome restrictions and scrutiny now confronting the nonprofit sector.

■ Fund Management

Ohio became the 39th state to adopt a new standard for managing endowments, known as the Uniform Prudent Management of Institutional Funds Act, commonly referred to as UPMIFA. By the end of 2009 only three states had not introduced or enacted this model legislation, making this *de facto* the new standard for nonprofit investment.

More information can be found at the Web site http://www.upmifa.org.

The act is a model, so enacted legislation can vary by state and requires careful study. It raises the bar of "standard of care" expected of nonprofit officials in three areas. At the same time, it gives nonprofits two new powers that, if not controlled, can tempt cash-strapped nonprofits to make short-term decisions that can lead to long-term harm.

Higher Standard of Care

First, in light of the substantial investment losses in 2008, nonprofits are reconsidering how they invest. Some are avoiding equity or foreign investments and concentrating in a single class, such as cash or bonds. But the standard requires diversification. To do otherwise the nonprofit must identify special circumstances and articulate specific purposes for the investment fund that together justify and warrant concentration rather than diversification.

Second, when a donor gives a large amount of stock, a piece of real estate, or other non-cash asset, some nonprofits are tempted to time the market by delaying selling the asset in hopes of a higher sales price. To counter this temptation, many nonprofits have policies that require prompt sale of all gifts and immediate investment of the cash proceeds according to the asset allocation policy of the institution. The act codifies this practice by requiring "within a reasonable time" that the institution "make and carry out decisions" regarding whether to hold or sell the gifted property.

Third, whenever large gifts are received, the statute requires the institution to "rebalance" the newly enlarged portfolio to comply in a reasonable time with its asset allocation and other investment policies. This requirement is especially notable in times when hard-hit nonprofits are wondering whether to get back in the market. In positive equity markets, nonprofits have the opposite tendency to ride their profits into excessive exposure to equities or other high-flying asset classes. The law is clear: The nonprofit must adhere to its asset allocation policy.

New Powers

Many nonprofits with small or newly established endowments have run into large investment losses that have reduced the market value of their endowed funds below the original value of the gift, called the corpus or historical market value. Under the old statute, this situation (often called being underwater) requires suspension of any withdrawals from the affected endowed fund, causing a sharp reduction in revenue and possibly operating deficits.

The first new power embodied in the act allows boards to make withdrawals from endowment funds that are underwater. This new authority creates a significant dilemma for boards facing difficult budgets and looming operating deficits. The statute only requires that withdrawal decisions be "prudent and in good faith."

Any hesitation about board members' liability in Ohio is further allayed by statutory provision of an "irrefutable presumption of prudence" as long as the withdrawal is less than 5 percent of the three-year quarterly moving average market value of the fund.

The model statute offered a twig of counterpressure by suggesting a "rebuttable presumption of imprudence" if the withdrawal from underwater funds were greater than 7 percent. Ohio, and several other states did not enact this countermeasure.

This new power is hazardous. It can make sense only when budget pressures would otherwise irreparably harm the mission of the organization. And even then, it is prudent only when the nonprofit has a solid plan and commitment to make the corpus whole from operating funds after the severe circumstances abate. The persistent pressure on most nonprofits to use excess operating resources to expand or improve services in good times makes one skeptical the corpus will ever be made whole so that the long-term value of the endowment would have been permanently eroded.

Finally, the act has given nonprofits a second new power to release gifts from donor restrictions. Until now, to change restrictions on gifts, nonprofits had to get the written permission from the donor or else begin a lengthy and costly legal process called *cy pres*. The act allows a nonprofit to unilaterally release or modify restrictions on small gifts made years earlier. Ohio enacted an easier standard than the model legislation: gifts of less than $250,000 made more than 10 years ago can be unilaterally modified. The nonprofit must only notify the state attorney general of its intent and attest that the intended use would still be consistent with the original charitable purpose of the gift.

Used with restraint, this new authority can allow nonprofits to tap myriad gifts whose restrictions have become antiquated, superseded, or extremely difficult to meet, and allow the funds to be used for purposes that are similar but were not apparent at the time of the gift.

On the other hand, without restraint this new power can foster distrust by current and future donors and undermine fundraising.

Overall, the new standard represents the lessons learned over the past 35 years. It tightens up where needed and it loosens up where flexibility can help nonprofits sustain their missions.

But this new authority requires enhanced internal discipline. Nonprofits would be wise to use these new powers cautiously and with restraint.

V. CRISIS OPPORTUNITIES

Financial crisis can happen to any nonprofit, no matter how well-managed. Responses to a financial crisis must always proceed on two tracks. One track, obviously, must be to preserve cash. The other track – the one less traveled – is objective, reflective research about what the crisis is telling you regarding the strengths and the weaknesses of the nonprofit organization.

Preservation of cash means accelerating the receipt of cash and delaying spending. It is critically important to make sure that spending reductions do not compromise the strategic priorities of the nonprofit. In crisis, the board and management need to work together with a division of labor that is consistent with their respective roles. Boards can be most helpful in outreach to donors to accelerate payment of pledges as well as to solicit new pledges. The choice of where to cut spending tempts many boards but it is the rare board member who has sufficient knowledge of the operations of the nonprofit to make wise cuts. Management should choose cuts and report with sufficient transparency that the board can assess that the strategic priorities of the nonprofit have been preserved as much as possible.

One can often emerge from crisis in a stronger position if one approaches a crisis as a massive influx of information to be digested as part of a re-evaluation of evolving community need, continued mission importance, and underlying business structure. This review must be a joint task of management and board. They must consciously counteract any desire to preserve routine and the status quo and instead view crisis as a mandate for thoughtful change. This is the time to charge a joint working group to think big and to consider adding and dropping programs, combining central office functions with other nonprofits, or even merger.

Communication must always be a key part of crisis management. Talking about your problems is not easy to do but, in combination with a clear description of how you are responding, it can reinforce donors' trust and confidence in the nonprofit and place philanthropy in the context of a partnership to work together to use the crisis to realign the nonprofit to better meet the current and future needs of the community.

■ Re-evaluation

Many nonprofits these days are encountering donors who are less willing or less able to provide support. Government support and contracts are harder to obtain or come with less generous terms. Earned income is flat or declining.

The big question is whether these troubles are temporary or symptomatic of a general decline in a community's need or support for the nonprofit's purpose?

If it is temporary or cyclical, the nonprofit needs only to survive until the economy turns around. But if the troubles are persistent or structural, the nonprofit will need to change how its raises money, how it spends money, or both.

Determining the true situation is tough because the search can be affected by two burdens that are acute for the nonprofit sector.

One is guilt that the community needs the nonprofit to do more and it must persist regardless of its circumstances.

The other is a reluctance to have faith in the judgments of its donors, clients, and patrons. These burdens are most difficult to overcome in times of economic decline.

Change is necessary

In contrast, profit-making companies are more willing to accept outsiders' judgments of their value by choosing to be sold, merge, or go out of business. Companies that were around 20 years ago are not the same ones around nowadays.

In the for-profit world we accept that people still have needs but over time they choose to address their needs in different ways.

Communities and the community needs that are addressed by the nonprofit sector are not so different – the needs still exist, but the community may choose to address the needs in different ways.

Honest look

In times of difficulty, it is essential that nonprofits remain open to messages from their supporters. While it is always gratifying to hear support for its purpose and what it accomplishes, the nonprofit mustn't disregard more worrisome messages or push away the friends who send those messages.

This situation is reminiscent of the tragedy of Shakespeare's *King Lear*. The king rejected his most loyal daughter, Cordelia, because she spoke the truth and refused to flatter him with unrealistic promises of support.

But it was Lear's other daughters, flattering him with specious love and loyalty, who tempted him to choose the path that led to his demise. At that point, even Cordelia was helpless to restore him to his former greatness.

These days many nonprofits are facing reductions in support from city and county governments. They are reeling from the United Way's sharp narrowing of what it will support. Are these budget actions the frank messages of loyal Cordelia? Are the urgings of others to stay the course empty promises that keep us on the road to greater difficulties?

The best course for a nonprofit is to listen to all these messages and respond by performing the same research and considering the same options available to for-profit companies.

Market research and surveys are critical reality tests of a non-profit group's actions and how much the community values it. If the community sees less value, then a nonprofit must purposefully identify changes that boost its value or reduce the level of activity.

At the same time, this research may identify needs that are unmet which the nonprofit can retool itself to provide. Merging with another nonprofit, dropping a service, or ceasing operations entirely are not actions of disloyalty to mission if the community need is no longer significant or is better met by another nonprofit.

As community needs vary over time, the nonprofits which are needed by the community will also vary.

Ears open

When a nonprofit is facing difficulty in finding enough funding, it is appropriate to seek out other nonprofits that do similar work to see if ceding the work to them or merging will best address the needs of the community at a level the community can afford. If not, no one should feel guilty proclaiming mission fulfilled and shutting down.

When facing such difficulties a well-run nonprofit will keep its ears open to messages of both praise and criticism, and it will use that information to guide objective, reflective research to determine if its troubles are due to the recession or to a structural change in its value to the community.

If King Lear had listened more carefully, the community would have been better off.

■ Necessity - The Mother of Invention

As layoffs mount and well-known corporations fail, many are asking how could this happen to such well-regarded institutions. Thoughtful policymakers are also questioning the effectiveness of CEOs and boards of directors in overseeing the financial risks and sustainability of their companies.

Management guru Peter Drucker in his book *Peter Drucker on nonprofit management* highlighted three areas in which successful nonprofits "are practicing what American businesses only preach." They are:

- Planning based on mission.

- Effective use of boards of directors.

- Motivation and productivity of knowledge workers.

Much of what he said remains relevant. Nonprofits should endeavor to exploit their potential advantage in these areas and for-profits would do well to consider how these approaches could improve their practices. While this suggestion may seem ironic to those who think nonprofits can't manage well, Drucker has the opposite sentiment: "The best nonprofits learned long ago that business is not a dirty word. In fact, because they lack the straightforward discipline of the for-profit bottom line, nonprofits know that they need good management even more than for-profit businesses do. [Nonprofits'] good intentions cannot substitute for accountability, performance, and results, which begin with good management."

Planning based on mission

For-profit management is complex, but it also is straightforward because of its necessary focus on financial results, a focus which nonprofits replace with the more difficult focus on mission.

Drucker says: "Starting with mission and its requirements focuses the organization on action and designing specific strategies needed to attain mission-critical goals. It can prevent the most degenerative disease of organizations, especially large ones: Splintering their always limited resources on things that look profitable rather than concentrating them on a very small number of productive efforts."

Successful nonprofits have learned to define clearly what impacts on the community constitute results and to focus on them.

A well-defined mission provides the discipline to measure a nonprofit's success in terms of its value in satisfying the community's needs rather than in terms of self-satisfaction based on the goodness of its cause.

Effective use of the board

Drucker believes that the most successful nonprofits find the root of their success in the boardroom.

He notes: "Many nonprofits have what is still the exception in business – a functioning board. They also have something even rarer: a CEO who is clearly accountable to the board and whose performance is reviewed annually by a board committee. The top managements of large companies have been whittling away at the directors' role, power, and independence for more than half a century. In every single business failure of a large company in the last few decades, the board was the last to realize that things were going wrong.

"While this began historically in the form of working nonprofit boards, the advent of professional nonprofit management has not rendered the nonprofit board impotent as many for-profit boards can become. Few directors in publicly held boards are substantial shareholders, whereas directors on nonprofit boards very often contribute large sums themselves, and have a personal commitment to the organization's cause. Precisely because the nonprofit board is so committed and active, this has forced an increasing number of nonprofits to realize that neither board nor CEO is the boss but rather colleagues working for the same goal but each having a different task."

Motivation and productivity

All nonprofits have their roots in unpaid volunteers. The need to attract, retain, and motivate volunteers has led the best-performing nonprofits to emphasize that volunteers and staff need to feel satisfaction from accomplishments and a sense of personal contribution.

Drucker explains why: "What do volunteers and staff demand? Their first and foremost demand is that the nonprofit have a clear mission, one that drives everything the organization does. The second thing they demand is training. And, in turn, the most effective way to motivate and hold veterans is to recognize their expertise and use them to train newcomers. Then these knowledge workers demand responsibility. They expect to be consulted and to participate in making decisions that affect their work and the work of the organization. And they expect opportunities for advancement. That is why a good many nonprofits have developed career ladders, for the volunteers as well as their staff."

Drucker summarizes the lessons for-profits can take from nonprofit best practices: "Managing the knowledge worker for productivity is the challenge ahead. The non-profits are showing us how to do that. It requires a clear mission, careful placement and continuous learning and teaching, management by objectives and self-control, high demands but corresponding responsibility, and account-ability for performance and results."

The best nonprofits have made a virtue out of necessity. They have forged tools that produce focused action-orient-ed strategies, maximize board contributions, and inspire the knowledge workers of tomorrow.

■ Critical Steps

Recent headlines in the nonprofit press read "Nonprofit Groups Struggle as Economic Crisis Spreads." This kind of news reminds us that all nonprofits are subject to the business cycle.

Indeed, nonprofit revenue historically declines during economic downturns and rises during economic recoveries. For some nonprofits, this effect is compounded by a surge in demand for their services during economic downturns. It's little surprise that some of the hardest hit nonprofits provide food, housing, financial counseling, and jobless support.

At the same time, and without exception, endowments decline when the economy falls. Endowment wealth does not inoculate nonprofits from the economy.

The only reliable protection is to build operating reserves during good times so that the nonprofit can sustain services during difficult times by using those reserves for operations. Building reserves means budgeting for surpluses, even when donors demand to see immediate results from their gifts.

Monitor weekly

Given the depth and breadth of the current economic decline, even the most prepared nonprofit managers must take steps to preserve their agencies' services. The first step is to monitor cash every week.

One good tool is a spreadsheet that lists anticipated cash receipts and anticipated bills by week, including payroll and related tax and benefit payments. Before approving any check run, use the spreadsheet to see if the unrestricted cash balance will go negative from that check run and identify any bills that can be deferred in order to preserve enough cash to pay other bills that are more essential to maintaining services. Reschedule the deferred bills to future weeks in which projected cash appears sufficient.

If this exercise indicates too many bills appear unpayable, then the nonprofit must move into cash crisis mode. Once a cash crisis has been identified, the board and senior management need to take immediate steps to stop or slow the momentum of spending and the drain on remaining cash.

These steps are designed to achieve three purposes:

- Buy time for the nonprofit to establish control over the current situation so it does not become a passive victim of events.

- Provide a tool to spot quickly the new problems which are highly likely to appear during a crisis.

- Initiate changes in reporting and governance to enhance the nonprofit's ability to anticipate problems and respond earlier when the next crisis occurs.

Being aware

Even when problems are well known, one must confront the tendency to continue routine purchasing, hiring, and contracting. Routine is most effectively disrupted by imposing an immediate freeze on purchasing and hiring. The purpose of a freeze is to buy time to identify and implement permanent spending changes. Any freeze must have exceptions, but they should be chosen carefully.

If your budget has made provision for inflationary increases, those increases should be immediately removed from the budget. All set-asides for future payments should be cancelled and restored only after careful review of the nonprofit's contractual obligations and the mission priority of the purchase.

While micromanagement must be avoided in normal times, the board and senior management must be vigilant and hands-on during a cash crisis so they can discern whether the disruption in spending is succeeding.

Detailed implementation plans need to be developed for major savings targets. This is most effective when staffers know their efforts are being closely monitored and that any effort to postpone the spending reductions will be foiled.

Even with close monitoring and spending freezes, a temporary cash shortfall may be unavoidable.

External financing may be obtainable through a line of credit with a bank or from a temporary loan from a major benefactor. Social services nonprofits that are facing serious cash-flow problems should investigate the nonprofit Finance Fund, which has recently introduced its Accounts Receivable Line of Credit program for those with cash-flow issues stemming from slow payments on government contracts. Eligibility in the program is limited and nonprofits should contact the Finance Fund directly.

Internal financing may be obtainable from restricted funds but note this: Any borrowing from restricted funds must be preceded by a credible plan that demonstrates the ability to restore that money before the end of the fiscal year.

Power of the public

It is counterproductive for a nonprofit to maintain public silence through crisis. Experience has taught that donors and supporters respond when they are promptly and regularly informed of the crisis and the response plan. That demands reaching out to the public and media. But the outreach should be limited to facts; avoid speculation or idle threats of worst-case spending cuts.

Once a way to slow spending has been implemented, short-term financing arranged, and a media effort undertaken, it is time for reflection and reform.

The nonprofit should first view the crisis as an opportunity to develop more effective ways to anticipate future problems. Reporting and monitoring processes should be re-evaluated.

It is also a useful time to decide how to manage differently during economic recovery in order to be in a stronger position when the next downturn occurs.

■ Mergers

The economy is slowing, financial markets are in disarray, and many donors are feeling pinched. This is a good time for nonprofit groups to critically evaluate how they will sustain services over the coming years. Can the nonprofit do it alone? Or, can it do better by collaborating or merging with another nonprofit?

Nonprofit trustees and officers should consider collaborations ranging from shared staff to shared space or equipment to shared back offices to a pure merger of the corporate entities.

There have been at least 10 mergers of nonprofits in Central Ohio in recent years and many more collaborations of varying scope. Opera Columbus and Columbus Children's Theater have joined to share the same building. FirstLink and the Columbus Literacy Council share a building, computer systems, and receptionists. CAPA shares the same administration with CATCO. CAPA also provides administrative and/or ticketing services to CATCO, Franklin Park Conservatory, Opera Columbus, and Columbus Children's Theater. Children's Hunger Alliance and New Directions share a joint lease. And GroundWork Group and CIVIC completed a merger, as did Faith Mission with Lutheran Social Services and CATCO with Phoenix Theater.

Lessons Learned

This experience in the Columbus area has provided some lessons.

First, in contrast with for-profit organizations, financial considerations are rarely a sufficient foundation for a successful nonprofit merger. If a nonprofit is in financial trouble, it is generally too late to seek solution through a merger because it has little to offer a potential partner other than its liabilities.

The experience in Central Ohio has been that a merger is successful when the impetus for the combination comes from both boards of directors of the potential partners. It is critical to overcome board reluctance because, without a board's commitment, mergers often aren't consummated.

The most opportune time to investigate collaboration or merger is when the mission is changing or when the mission no longer meets the needs of the community.

The investigation should look for ways that a merger or collaboration can provide an opportunity to do things an agency could not do otherwise or do as efficiently or expeditiously. The board needs to see that the organization won't lose the niche it has historically filled.

Melding the habits and culture of staff, volunteers, and boards is typically the biggest challenge. One reason is that collaboration or merger is like starting a new job without it being a new job. Cultural issues can be as basic as the format of board meetings or even where the coffee pot is located.

How do you adjust the culture at multiple locations? How do you consolidate when the separate spaces were very different in neighborhood, spaciousness, or quality?

It is invaluable to have an independent third party that can look at the situation dispassionately and is willing to air all of the potential sticking points in an up-front manner. It is also essential to identify and confront territoriality.

The final lesson is that the first year should be viewed as a transitional year before the new board or system takes over from the two current boards or systems. The year should be totally devoted to dealing with the transition and shouldn't be burdened with new programs or new directions.

Help Available

Helpful background and insights on the range of possible collaborations and the issues most often encountered can be found in Amelia Kohn and David La Piana's study, "Strategic Restructuring for Nonprofit Organizations."

Money to help nonprofits investigate possible mergers or collaborations are available. The United Way of Central Ohio and the Columbus Foundation have competitive grant programs for capacity building, which can provide funds for consultants, training, and other support to help nonprofits investigate the feasibility of collaborations and mergers. Staff at both organizations are available to talk about the value, feasibility, and potential hurdles of particular collaborations or mergers the nonprofits may be considering.

■ Corporate Giving

In the current economy, a for-profit company may be experiencing unprecedented declines in sales and access to capital markets. As it looks for ways to preserve cash it is understandable that it is re-examining its philanthropic support of nonprofits.

Some companies are consolidating their giving programs by dropping some nonprofits altogether while maintaining their historic level of support for each retained nonprofit organization. Others are continuing to support the same number of nonprofits but at a uniformly reduced level. And some companies are making no changes to their corporate giving, while other companies are dropping entire categories of nonprofits from their programs.

It is critical that reductions in corporate giving not be approached as a mathematical budget exercise. Rather, reductions should be considered in the context of the strategy that prompted the company to begin a giving program.

Was the program created for corporate visibility or public relations purposes? Is it part of a marketing program? Is it an extension of employee philanthropic preferences? Is it designed to enhance the appeal of the community to potential job candidates?

Communicate

If your company's strategy regarding giving to nonprofits has not been clearly articulated, it is important to do so before making any changes in giving.

Strategy is important because the first decision in revising your giving program must be to decide if the changes are temporary in response to immediate financial pressures or if they are permanent and represent a change in your giving strategy. This distinction is critical in determining the best ways to determine how you reduce your giving.

Temporary changes should be designed to mitigate the disruption to the nonprofits which you support.

The worst outcome would be for temporary changes to your program to create lasting effects that will compromise your ability to restore the program to what it is today. Examples of lasting effects would be the cancellation of a service program, the elimination of entire categories of funding recipients, or the failure of a nonprofit you would otherwise continue to support.

Permanent changes should be designed to establish a new strategy that will form the basis for future giving once your company's financial situation improves.

Examples of changes in strategy would be changes in which nonprofits you support and changes in how you provide support, such as general operating support, program grants, cost reimbursement contracts, matching grants, or start-up funds.

This new strategy should be clearly articulated so that nonprofits who will remain part of your strategy can plan appropriately, and nonprofits who will not remain in your program will remove expectations of future support from their planning.

Temporary Cutbacks

It is most likely that you are changing your giving program in response to current business conditions, which will eventually turn around. In this case, your changes are temporary.

You should carefully design changes that respond to your current financial circumstances with the least impact on nonprofits' ability to sustain themselves and their mission. If these changes are temporary for you, the nonprofits you support will be best off if they can find responses that also are temporary. For them to have the best chance of doing this, they will need to have as much time and flexibility as possible to develop responses.

Here are five interrelated principles to guide your temporary reduction decisions.

Don't delay decisions. Nonprofits need time to assemble responses. The more time you take to make your decisions, the less time they have to react.

It is a false expectation that taking more time for your decisions will result in a better outcome for the nonprofits. Responsible nonprofits will have to interpret your delay in deciding what you will give as a decision to give nothing. Any other response would be reckless.

It is obvious that your financial situation will improve; however, you cannot predict when that will occur. So make your decisions now on the basis of what you know now.

Be explicit about whether this is a temporary or a permanent change in your giving program. It may be obvious to you whether your reductions in nonprofit support are temporary or permanent, but it is not obvious to the nonprofits you have been supporting.

Nonprofits survive based on optimism, so they are inclined to treat your reduction as temporary. A misunderstanding on this point could prove fatal to a nonprofit.

Also, if you believe this is a temporary reduction, make sure your senior management concurs and, if possible, get it in writing with some understanding of what circumstances will allow this temporary reduction to be reversed.

Don't create false hope. Community relations staff invest a lot of time and effort in creating good relations with nonprofits.

Giving out news of reductions in support is no different than giving out layoff notices. It is vital that you communicate your reductions frankly and not hedge.

Don't speculate about the possibility of more support later in the year; it may make you feel better, but it may mislead the nonprofits enough for them to craft responses that will lead to dire circumstances if your aid increase does not materialize.

Be mindful of the implications on nonprofit fiscal year results. Nonprofits are under enormous pressure to show budget balance in their fiscal year results.

Regardless of your views on this, too many grantors evaluate the quality of nonprofit management based on balancing the budget. If the nonprofits you support are on a June 30 fiscal year, providing your support before June 30 has substantially more value than providing it later.

Even though you are decreasing the amount of your support, if your nonprofit giving program has flexibility in the timing of payments, writing your check earlier will mitigate the impact of the reduction. If you are unsure of their fiscal year situations, ask them.

Know the cashflow implications of how you provide support. Many nonprofits have weak balance sheets so that cash is very tight and making payroll is a constant challenge. You can mitigate the impact of your reduction in support by changing the criteria for support.

Now is a good time to reconsider match requirements, which make your support unavailable unless and until the nonprofit can come up with matching cash. In this environment, requiring a match substantially reduces and may jeopardize the ability of a nonprofit to use your support.

Similarly, if you provide support through reimbursement, you are writing your check after the nonprofit has already had to come up with the cash. By giving them your check before they incur the related expenses you will help their cashflow and partially offset the impact of your reduced support.

Better yet, make your gift unrestricted so that they can keep your support even if they decide their best response to reduced giving must be to suspend the program you have been supporting.

Reducing your support of nonprofits is unfortunate but sometimes necessary when the economy weakens. Prompt decision-making, explicit communication, and enhancing flexibility in the timing and usefulness of your giving may be a silver lining in this otherwise cloudy outlook.

VI. CHALLENGES IN PHILANTHROPY

Philanthropy and fundraising have become a business. Like any business, it has challenges of identity.

- Is a philanthropist a manager of community services or a writer of checks?

- Does the philanthropy support programs or does it support nonprofit organizations?

- Does a philanthropist trust that his gifts to nonprofits have value or does he need proof of that value?

- Is the philanthropist an investor who expects a return or does he give because it is the right thing to do?

- Is generosity achieved by planned giving? by endowment giving? by annual giving? by restricted giving?

This identify struggle creates tensions with the nonprofit community that need to be acknowledged and openly discussed.

In addition, the weak economy has coincided with a precipitous decline in giving – and much of the giving that remains is restricted and unavailable to support much of the necessary infrastructure any viable business needs in order to be effective. This trend has led to a crisis of sustainability for many important nonprofits, particularly in the arts and culture sector.

Part of the problem is the blurring of the line between donor and manager. Are grants gifts or are they contracts managed by the grantor? The answer to this question depends on who has the most knowledge about what the community needs and the most effective way to address that need. Historically, donors trusted the nonprofit to have the better expertise. Nowadays the restrictions in gifts and grants imply that the donor believes he knows best and the nonprofit is an implementer. To restore trust, nonprofits must have a clear, objective, transparent assessment of changing community needs along with an effective and persuasive strategy to address those needs. Trust can be restored only when fundraisers start to sell a solution to a compelling problem rather than ask for money to cover deficits.

Thirty years ago the federal government provided many services directly and fully covered the cost. Over the ensuing decades, many services have been shifted to state and local governments without sufficient federal funds to cover the cost. The resulting state and local budget pressures led to a similar shift onto the nonprofits. In the current economic crisis, state and local governments have been reluctant to lay off government workers and have balanced their budgets by reducing or slowing their payments to the nonprofits. Nonprofits, therefore, are increasingly the providers of last resort for key public services. The expectation that nonprofits will maintain key services while governmental and philanthropic support declines is a recipe for failure of the nonprofit sector and for erosion of the services our society deems essential to its wellbeing.

This section was placed near the end of the book in the hopes that the preceding sections have provided insight into the importance of human nature and common sense in nonprofit decision-making. With the benefit of this insight, it is hoped you can better understand the provocative theme of this section: recent trends in the way philanthropists and governments are doing good have the potential to undermine the vitality and effectiveness – and in some cases the survival – of nonprofits.

■ Blurring the Lines between Donor and Manager

There are three emerging trends in philanthropy that are well-intentioned but can have unintended adverse consequences for nonprofits.

If a harmful effect may be emerging, it is vitally important for nonprofit managers and their boards to engage donors in meaningful conversation on how the good intentions can be retained while minimizing the potential for harm. These three trends are:

- Philanthropy focused on seed funds, seed grants, or start-up funding.

- Philanthropy that requires matching funds.

- Philanthropy that requires the measurement of outcomes and quantitative evidence of positive effects.

Seed grants

Seed grants are made to support a new undertaking for two to three years with the expectation that the nonprofit will develop new sources of earned or donated funding to replace the seed grant money. The intention is to provide a source of scarce investment funding so nonprofits can afford to take on new challenges or approach old problems in new ways. This is laudable.

But as this type of grant becomes more prevalent, the flip side of the coin is that nonprofits are sent a strong signal that growth is necessary to attract donors. Not only can growth turn a successful nonprofit into a troubled one, the pressure created by seed grants can also subtly push nonprofits toward programs that can be supported with fees and charges.

Indeed, there is an emerging view that nonprofits that are 60 percent fee-supported and 40 percent donor-supported, for example, are better managed than those that have donated money supporting 50, 60, 70 percent or more of expenses. We need to remind ourselves that sometimes the current programs are the right programs to support and that nonprofits were created because community need could not be paid for with fees and charges.

Matching grants

Matching or challenge grants are made either to provide an incentive to other donors or to ensure the grantor that the nonprofit is committed to the program as evidenced by its willingness to "put skin in the game." This type of philanthropy is beneficial if it attracts new donors or encourages existing donors to increase the size of their gifts (this is called leveraging).

On the other hand, when matching or challenge grants are directed to specific programs, they can weaken the nonprofit financially.

A nonprofit must be wary of matching gift programs forcing its fundraisers to shift part of their effort to the area supported by the matching gift and away from other areas needing support. In the extreme, matching gift programs can implicitly force unrestricted giving into restricted categories.

In a world of scarce donor dollars, nonprofit executives need to preserve the unrestricted support of their core programs and their administrative systems. If a matching or challenge grant has the potential to divert fundraising away from unrestricted operating support, a nonprofit executive and board must try to change the terms of the grant or consider turning it down.

Performance measurement

Performance measurement is a useful management tool that is increasingly required by donors. Donors have expropriated this management tool as a way to measure the effectiveness of their giving.

The potential danger of performance measurement lies in the presumption that a benefit exists only when the benefit can be quantified or a problem can be solved.

In many cases, nonprofits are asked to deal with the community's most intractable problems. One must remain open-minded that the mission of a nonprofit can have merit – and merit support – even if an outcome or an improvement cannot be measured quantitatively. Do we help a child in reading only if the child's reading scores improve? Do we help a homeless person only if he gets a job or moves into permanent housing? Do we support the arts only if audiences increase or community value can be quantified?

There is merit to feeding the hungry, helping troubled youth, housing the homeless, tutoring a child, producing art, and making music even when a problem isn't solved or we can't quantify improvement.

Let Good Managers Manage

Just as we need good nonprofit managers to be business-like, the community also needs good nonprofit donors to support the decisions of good nonprofit managers. Trying to influence nonprofit managers through restrictions or limitations or quantitative reporting is not effective philanthropy.

In a previous chapter we referenced Jim Collins' concern that donors applying their for-profit behaviors on nonprofits can undermine good decision-making by nonprofits. With this in mind, nonprofit managers need to examine with caution any gift or grant that provides starter funds, calls for a match, or requires quantitative measures of outcomes.

Visualize what your nonprofit might become five to 10 years from now if these conditions were to be the norm. If you see the potential for adverse, albeit unintended, effects, talk to your donors and think twice before accepting that gift.

It is difficult to challenge a donor, just as it is difficult for a for-profit executive to challenge a major investor. But your nonprofit exists to meet a community need and you owe it to your community to help donors support your approach to mission.

■ Provider of Last Resort

Local governments are holding hearings about the services local taxes will fund. Nonprofit groups providing a wide range of services are seeing the support they have traditionally received from local governments come under challenge.

This is the latest stage of a process that began two decades ago when the federal government began outsourcing public services to private organizations and shifting funding obligations onto state governments. Known popularly as unfunded mandates, these obligations moved down to local governments over the past decade and now they are moving further down to the nonprofit sector.

It is time to review what has happened and to ponder its consequences.

This logical endpoint of outsourcing and unfunded mandates would have the nonprofit sector be a major provider of public services and potentially a major funder as well. Ironically, the nonprofit sector is confronted with being cast as the provider of last resort for a wide range of services that economics tells us should be provided by the government.

The core of the problem lies in the economic concepts of public goods and free riders. Public goods are those goods and services whose benefit extends beyond the person paying for them. Free riders are people who receive these indirect benefits but do not help to pay for them.

A park benefits the visitor and indirectly the neighborhood. Education indirectly benefits the employer, who gets skilled employees, and the public, which gets additional taxpayers and consumers who will contribute to the economy. A vibrant downtown indirectly benefits the suburbanite who may rarely come downtown. Homeless shelters and food pantries indirectly benefit the public by preserving neighborhoods and alleviating social unrest. Free clinics and emergency rooms indirectly benefit the public by reducing the risk of spread of disease.

The gradual shifting of obligations from the federal government down to the states, and ultimately down to the local governments, favors the free riders – those states, municipalities, and individuals who don't want to pay for the indirect benefits of these services. Many of these services are now provided by nonprofit organizations. Art, music, counseling, tutoring, sports, and after-school activities have shifted out of the public schools and into nonprofits. Emergency housing, food, healthcare, and homecare are also increasingly provided by nonprofits.

The next step is the expectation that the nonprofits will pick up the funding burden as well.

While outsourcing to the nonprofit sector is a legitimate option for providing public services, shifting funding of more public services to the nonprofit sector is a worrisome trend for two reasons.

The economic concern is that the amount of these public goods and services will be insufficient and society will be less well off if free riders are allowed to benefit without paying. Economists conclude that the proper level of services is best provided through mandatory taxes on all who directly or indirectly benefit. As the number of people benefiting expands, the level of government providing and taxing for the public good or service should move from the city to the county to the state and ultimately to the federal government. In contrast, the events of past decades have shifted the burden from all citizens to volunteer citizens, from taxpayers to the smaller set of nonprofit donors.

The business concern is that donors nowadays are less willing to provide operational funding and nonprofits are already so poorly capitalized that they have limited or no ability to sustain services. Thus, as we see the clouds of economic recession above us, those public services we most need in a recession may have a poorer chance of being available.

Nonprofits are committed to their missions and they will work hard to provide public services in the face of reduced governmental support. But given the benefits we all directly and indirectly receive from the services they provide, is it in the public's interest to rely more heavily on nonprofits' success in getting donors to write the checks that we don't want to ask taxpayers to write?

■ More than a Party

Galas are the most visible fund-raising activity of nonprofits. Intended as a thank you to donors and a celebration of everything positive about the organization, galas are becoming so popular that major donors can easily have one a week at peak times of the year.

Before you plan your next gala, I have a suggestion: Ask your major donors what they most want from you. Don't be surprised if their answer is: "What's most important to us is not your party but your effort to keep us well-informed of what you are doing and how you are doing financially."

In a certain sense, a major donor or grantor is in a position very similar to a board member of a nonprofit. They both have committed to the mission, one by joining the board and the other by providing a significant gift.

They both believe there is an effective plan to link money to the nonprofit's mission, the board by approving the budget and the donor by writing the check. They both need to know the plan is being executed well, the board by regular meetings and reports and the donor by …. And there may lie a problem: After making the gift, donors may not hear back until they get an invitation to the next fundraiser.

Donors need regular, understandable information to carry out their job to know their generosity is effective and getting a reasonable bang for the buck.

Major donors need financial information that is clearly presented in the context of your community's needs, your mission to fulfill those needs, your goals and priorities in directing the use of funds, and your assessment and measurement of your achievements. Simply mailing them a newsletter, an annual financial report or a Form 990 federal tax return doesn't meet this need. The nonprofit board should already receive information that objectively (and persuasively, of course) lets the board know the organization's needs, condition and performance. You should share that information with donors.

Insight for contributors

Informing donors the way you inform your board can bring enormous benefits. Providing that same format, that same document that the board regularly sees will enhance the impression that you are telling it like it is – no varnish, no spin, and no skeletons in the closet.

Individual major donors may not have staffs and they may be the most appreciative of your ability to explain your financial situation in a concise and non-technical manner. This idea of full and regular disclosure may make some nonprofits uncomfortable. After all, even in the best of organizations, there are spots that aren't performing as well as others, so the idea of providing board-level information to donors may strike some as unduly advertising the warts and potentially undermining donor confidence in the nonprofit.

But remember, donors already believe nonprofits are doing something that no one else has been doing or has been able to do. Donors don't expect nonprofits to be perfect; they expect them to be competent, committed, and careful with donors' money. Keeping donors informed is the only convincing way to meet these expectations.

Try it with one of your donors. You may find the benefits great enough to set aside your worries.

Back to the party

If information is more important to donors, you may want to reconsider the rationale for your gala. Does the gala truly raise extra funds and attract new donors or does it instead divert scarce donor time and money to the event? Donors, or the staff representing donors, increasingly see work encroaching on family time, and the evenings that galas occupy can take a steep toll.

In terms of bang for the buck, a gala may not always be the most effective investment. Because a gala provides benefits like food, drinks and entertainment, a $10,000 table is not fully tax-deductible to the donor. Considering staff time and including expenses, the benefit to the nonprofit may be $7,000 or less.

If you skipped the gala and asked for a $8,500 check instead, the nonprofit's net benefit would likely be higher than from the gala table and the donor's after-tax cost would likely be lower than from buying a table. More benefit, smaller check, one more evening free. This may be a win-win worth considering.

In the meantime, focus on keeping your donors informed. If you still want to have a party, you and your donors will at least have more to talk about than the food.

■ Donor's Trust

Some popular forms of philanthropy need special vigilance if they are to have the intended, positive effect on nonprofits. Among these are seed grants, matching grants, performance measurement, and the fondness for gifts to go into endowment.

What these forms of philanthropy have in common is that they are gifts with strings attached. While many motives for attaching strings are possible, I am most concerned that one motive is a simple lack of trust between donor and nonprofit.

In a recent talk before fundraising professionals I was asked, "What do I do about a donor who says he trusts the current management but isn't sure the future management will be good, so he wants to put restrictions on his gift or put it into endowment." The donor's restriction was that the principal of the gift could never be spent.

Everyone is familiar with the term fiduciary, a person who stands in a special relation of trust, confidence, or responsibility. The word derives from the Latin word *fidere*, which means "to trust." In a nonprofit, that special responsibility is to the organization's mission. I would take that one step further: The foremost responsibility of a fiduciary is to *sustain* mission.

Owner-client confusion

Nonprofits are given special legal status because they have a mission that meets a community need that the market and the for-profit sector are not able or willing to meet. The community and its citizens build their lives around having that mission fulfilled by the nonprofit. They rely on that mission being sustained through good times and bad.

Thus, a fiduciary's duty is to see that citizens' trust in the nonprofit's sustainability is honored.

Don't donors, especially large donors, have a special relationship to their beneficiaries that rises to the level of having a fiduciary duty to use their philanthropy to sustain the nonprofit's mission?

John Carver brought the path-breaking insights of Policy Governance® to the board-staff relationship when he examined the fiduciary role of boards of trustees. Carver is famous for asking who is the owner and who is the client. A donor can be both owner and client, making Carver's question even more trenchant.

As Carver points out, how can a donor possibly have greater knowledge and skill to sustain a nonprofit's mission than the nonprofit's managers have with their full-time, on-site, everyday involvement? The answer to Carver's question cannot be that donors should fulfill their accountability by attaching strings to their gifts!

Jim Collins, in *Good to Great and the Social Sectors*, came to a similar insight: Donors imposing their preferences can undermine the culture of discipline that enables a nonprofit to maintain the laser focus on sustaining mission that is necessary for a nonprofit to move from good to great.

Perhaps the most effective donors are not defined by the restrictions or requirements they impose but rather by their support of the nonprofit's mission and their trust that the nonprofit knows best how to use their gifts to address and sustain the mission. The answer to Carver's question surely must be that a donor fulfills his accountability by giving to the nonprofits he trusts or by engaging in committed dialogue with a nonprofit in order to establish trust.

Trust now, later

As a manager of a nonprofit, how you raise funds, what restrictions you accept, and whether those monies go into unrestricted accounts or into endowment accounts are the most central decisions you make in carrying out your fiduciary duties. In talking with donors, remind them that the purpose of their gift is to enhance the sustainability of your mission. Your sustainability is best enhanced when you have the financial flexibility that only unrestricted gifts can provide.

That brings us back to the question the fundraiser asked me the other day. Try this answer: When a donor says he trusts the current management but worries about how good future management will be, remind him that your nonprofit fulfilled its mission 10, 20, or 30 years ago and it is fulfilling its mission now, so what is the reason to believe that will change?

If the donor doesn't feel that trust, rather than just accepting restrictions on the gift, probe what is the cause of his distrust and ask him what you *both* can do to establish that trust. Then make re-establishing that trust a top priority.

Down deep, the best gift that donors can give is the trust the nonprofit will use their money in the most effective manner possible.

■ Fundraising Planning

I recently received an email from a nonprofit board member asking for advice on designing a fundraising program. She noted the organization's funding was too dependent on weather-related events and asked whether it should focus on endowment and planned giving.

A nonprofit board's first duty is to be a reliable provider of a service that fulfills its mission. Fulfilling that duty has a clear prioritization: Assuring sustainability over the next year must come before sustainability over the next five years, which must be assured before tackling sustainability over the next 50 years. The key question is how do endowments and planned giving fit into these priorities?

Dealing with endowments

Raising an endowment is a decision to tap today's donors to provide resources for the distant future. The first rule of an endowment is that the original gift, the corpus, should not be spent. The second rule is that sufficient income must be set aside each year to maintain the inflation-adjusted value of the corpus. Only the income that is left over is intended to be used to support current operations of the organization. As a general rule, that support is about 5 percent of the endowment and it usually cannot begin much before the third year after the gift is made.

Consider this math: A donor who could give $10,000 to be used today is asked to give $10,000 that can never be spent, which will not produce spendable income for the next three years, and thereafter may be able to provide $500 per year to offset the effects of poor weather on event revenue. When dependency on revenue from weather-related events is a problem, its best funding solutions will enhance its ability to maintain services through a month, or a year, of weather-foiled events.

The endowment strategy does not solve this problem. Even if that donor were persuaded to make an extraordinary $30,000 endowment gift, the organization can expect future annual income of only $1,500. And in order to make that extraordinary gift, that donor may need to reduce annual giving below his customary $10,000. A potential reduction in near-term annual giving in exchange for endowment income of zero for up to three years and $1,500 thereafter?

Diverting an annual gift of $10,000 to a large endowment gift can be beneficial only if this organization can afford big fluctuations in weather and in annual giving. Since apparently it cannot, the nonprofit should instead be raising money that can be used immediately. An extraordinary gift of $30,000 could be highly beneficial, however, if it is placed in a board-designated reserve that can be tapped whenever an event is foiled by weather.

Dilemma of planned giving

Planned giving is an excellent program to provide for the very distant future. The bequests that come from these programs are uncertain in the timing and amount of monies that are eventually received.

One client of mine received its money 70 years after the bequest was established. Wills and bequests are easily changed over the years, and it is difficult for an organization to ever know how many wills provide for the organization, the gift in the original will, and whether changes have subsequently been made to the will.

It is best for an organization never to plan to receive a bequest so it can be pleasantly surprised when one arrives.

From this perspective, planned giving is irrelevant to the organization's problem with its vulnerability to weather-dependent events.

Planned giving campaigns do not happen on their own, and they have the potential to divert effort from annual fundraising.

The potential for a very large gift decades from now is difficult to evaluate against the need for continued modest gifts today.

If a nonprofit has enough staff, focusing on a planned giving program can make sense. But if it is struggling to balance annual budgets and maintain stable annual revenue, it must devote all available fundraising capacity to annual giving.

A nonprofit that needs to stabilize its funding and protect itself from the vicissitudes of weather-dependent events must focus its fundraising on programs that address this problem. Building working capital and accumulating a board designated rainy day reserve may be the best solutions to this problem. A fundraising campaign that solves these near-term problems can then move on to the problems that endowments and planned giving can solve.

■ Funding Restrictions

Too many nonprofits are grasshoppers. We need to let them be ants.

Everyone is familiar with the tale of the grasshopper and the ant. The grasshoppers focused on the day while the ants toiled to put away food for the coming winter. When winter came, the grasshoppers were starving while the ants were distributing food from the stores they had collected over the summer.

The moral of the story, of course, is that one should prepare for days of necessity. Nonprofits prepare for days of necessity by building flexibility and liquidity usually through accumulation of large, unrestricted cash reserves.

Unfortunately, we make it very hard for nonprofits to become ants all the while we are critical of their grasshopper-like vulnerability.

A common viewpoint is that nonprofits should manage themselves more like for-profit companies. I have always felt uneasy that this view ignored something very fundamental.

Recently, I came upon a paper by Clara Miller in the *Non-Profit Quarterly* that clarified my unease. The nub of her argument is the observation that when we invest in for-profit companies we give them our money for any purpose they choose.

Yet when we invest in nonprofits we tend to give the money with many restrictions on how and when the money can be spent, thereby limiting the value of the investment. The result is that restricted gifts make building flexibility and liquidity more expensive for a nonprofit, forcing many to remain grasshoppers, using far too many resources in the summer and leaving themselves stretched thin and vulnerable during the winter.

Unforeseen burdens

Restricted gifts have limited flexibility or liquidity and, in some circumstances, they can harm existing flexibility and liquidity.

For example, a nonprofit manager who receives a $50,000 gift restricted to a new exhibit cannot use this investment to boost attendance, increase working capital, upgrade computer systems, respond to unanticipated events, or add fundraising staff. Typically, the expanded program from that exhibit will also increase illiquid receivables, raise payables, probably add more illiquid assets requiring maintenance, and expand operating expenses.

To stay financially healthy with these changes, the nonprofit will need more unrestricted income and higher cash reserves than it did before accepting the restricted gift and adding the exhibit. Similarly, a restricted challenge grant requires fundraising staff to be diverted to raising funds for the restricted grant rather than for current operations.

Donors need to understand that restricted gifts have hidden costs – financial and nonfinancial. Some government and foundation programs acknowledge this by adding an extra payment for some of these extra costs, but generally corporate and individual donors do not compensate for the burden of their restrictions.

A nonprofit that wants to be an ant that is prepared for the winter needs to take one or more of the following five actions:

- Have strong seasonal ups and downs? Form an adequate working capital fund.

- Dependent on developing new programs? Form a reserve for program development.

- Have volatile revenue? Form a stabilization reserve.

- Are service demands unpredictable? Create an emergency service reserve.

- Have facilities or equipment that are essential to your operations? Create a maintenance and replacement reserve.

Paradox with dollar sign

This list is not a luxury; rather, it is an essential element for flexible and efficient management.

Yet it is difficult to fund because all these categories require unrestricted, liquid assets. Endowments, sponsorships, scholarship funds, matching gifts and other restricted gifts will generally make it more difficult to meet these needs.

Therein lies the paradox of nonprofit fundraising: As donors we want the biggest bang for the buck, yet we put restrictions on our investments in nonprofits that may wind up creating the need for bigger bucks for that same bang.

How can we expect nonprofits to achieve the flexibility and liquidity needed to prepare for difficult times when we routinely confront them with the hidden costs of restrictions we place on how they can use our gifts? As long as donors feel the need for restrictions, nonprofits will have one hand tied behind their backs and they will need increasing philanthropy in order to survive.

We trust for-profits to use our investments wisely; let's treat our nonprofits the same way and give unrestricted cash that they can use to build the reserves they need to sustain their current operations and become ants that are prepared for the winter.

■ Tax Write-offs

Robert Reich, former U.S. Secretary of Labor, set off a firestorm in the nonprofit world by challenging the motives for, and tax deductibility of, charitable contributions to higher education and culture.

"I see why a contribution to, say, the Salvation Army should be eligible for a charitable deduction. It helps the poor. But why exactly should a contribution to the already extraordinarily wealthy Guggenheim Museum or to Harvard University (which has an endowment of more than $30 billion)?" he asked.

"They're often investments in the lifestyles the wealthy already enjoy...They're also investments in prestige – especially if they result in the family name being engraved on the new wing of an art museum or symphony hall," he said.

The government's purpose for creating charitable deductions in the last century was to create an incentive to provide for a community need that the market economy could not or would not provide.

The Internal Revenue Service lists 12 community needs eligible for charitable deductions. Advancement of education and combating juvenile delinquency are two of the needs that higher education and our cultural institutions certainly address.

While Reich raises useful questions, he paints with too wide a brush. The two legitimate questions are narrower:

- What is the motive for giving and does the gift benefit the community at large?

- Stated another way, how far has philanthropic practice moved from the 19th century concept of selflessly and anonymously giving up private wealth for public ends by supporting a charitable organization with unrestricted giving?

As for the motive for giving, nonprofits groups can be accused of being overly zealous in using "naming opportunities" and "donor benefits" to attract donors. Reversing this trend will be important, but it poses a challenge for nonprofits.

As for supporting community need, philanthropy in recent years has steadily moved toward restricted giving, the troubling practice in which the donor specifies what the gift may be spent on, as well as toward performance measurement, in which the gift is viewed as an investment that must generate a return. The peril of this development is that the donor now decides what benefits the community.

But Reich goes too far in accusing universities and cultural institutions of not being "real charities."

The U.S. economy has been steadily shifting toward service industries. As a result, middle income salaries are increasingly achievable only with post-secondary education.

Yet only 27.2 percent of U.S. adults over age 25 had a bachelor's degree or higher in 2006. For that same year the Census Bureau found that average income for a householder with a bachelor's degree or more was $41,068 compared with $20,479 for one with a high school diploma.

Unambiguously, the community benefit from higher education is enormous.

Cultural institutions also provide huge community benefit, as has been amply documented by the Columbus Cultural Leadership Consortium and Americans for the Arts. The 16 largest cultural organizations in Central Ohio typically attract visitors from every county in Ohio, from 40 states and 30 countries. They engage 18,000 volunteers and provided programming to over 1 million students. They also provide professional development and continuing education programming to more than 4,000 teachers. The consortium's report, *Arts and Culture in Columbus, Creating Competitive Advantage and Community Benefit,* provides research evidence of the value of the arts to student achievement through higher test scores, lower dropout rates, and greater academic recognition.

Perhaps the relevant message from Reich is that we mustn't pay all our attention to the nonprofits that excel at fundraising and instead should make sure we also favor ones that aren't so good at asking for money.

And we should remember that the original purpose of philanthropy was to support a good cause and not expect anything in return.

■ Sustainability

A good indication of the stress in the nonprofit sector is talk of fiscal sustainability. One step forward in this discussion was a symposium held at Harvard University titled "Capital Ideas: Moving from Short-Term Engagement to Long-Term Sustainability."

The symposium proceedings reported that a large part of the problem comes from the pressure to address critical social issues so rapidly that the volume of service overwhelms the nonprofits' capacity. Money and effort become focused on results, leaving little or no cash for reserves or investment back into the organization.

A vivid example of this short-term focus is some nonprofits' boast that 100 percent of a donated dollar goes to service delivery.

Melissa Berman, of Rockefeller Philanthropy Advisors, said private donors steer clear of supporting sustainability because of what she labels misunderstanding, mistrust, and mismatch. The misunderstanding is about how the nonprofit sector works, which makes donors feel vulnerable to being snookered and wanting to understand where their money is going. Because donors cannot understand the nonprofit context, their mistrust leads them toward program support, which they think they can understand. The mismatch of power compels many nonprofits to acquiesce to private donors' whims. By way of illustration, Ms. Berman reports one recent comment by a donor: "I don't want to have to pay for light bulbs; somebody else should pay for light bulbs."

Emerging Models

There is a sense among donors that some changes in how philanthropy works in the U.S. would be beneficial. The symposium conducted a survey of 82 foundations which revealed four areas of strong agreement:

- Virtually all agreed foundation relationships with grantees should change from oversight to partnership.

- Virtually all saw the need to simplify grant applications and to scale back grantee effort to be more in line with the size and scope of particular grants.

- A sizable majority felt that grants should have fewer line items and restrictions and that donors should increase the size and length of grants.

- Most also felt that standardization of applications and reporting was desirable.

Movement in this direction already is occurring with some enlightened donors. Venture Philanthropy Partners in Washington, DC views its gifts as investments. It funds only infrastructure. Its average investment is $2.75 million and lasts 4.5 years. It has already concluded that future investments should be in the seven to 10 year range.

Similarly, the MacArthur Foundation has shifted $5 million of its grant program exclusively to multiyear operating support.

5 rules, 4 principles

The symposium recommended nonprofits could enhance their sustainability if donors would use these rules:

1. Equity is as important to nonprofits as it is to for-profit organizations. In the United States, public and private

donors focus on programs rather than on the organization. By contrast, the international donor world is seeing support of the organization as the key to sustainability.

2. Donors need to understand how their gifts blend with other donors' gifts in terms of risk level, term, disbursement rate, and purpose in order to assess how well their donations enhance the matching of resources.

3. Nonprofits need to know how cash moves through their entire organization and donors need to understand how their gifts can best support good cash management by the nonprofit.

4. All gifts should have some measure of return so the return can be consistent with the size, duration, and scope of the gift.

5. Performance measurement needs to focus on improvement rather than on the mistaken notion that benchmarks can measure effectiveness or excellence.

The proceedings of this symposium are excellent reading for anyone interested in fostering a healthy nonprofit sector and enhancing the value and effectiveness of philanthropy. A good place to start would be to ask how your community might benefit if donors and nonprofits agreed to build a relationship around these principles:

• Reduce the transaction costs nonprofits and donors incur from existing approaches to applying for and reporting on grants.

- Fund at the organizational level rather than the program level, even when the donor's or nonprofit's primary interest is in one program.

- Fund to meet the organization's business needs and operating realities.

- Small can be beautiful: Do not encourage growth for growth's sake.

■ Supply Chain Management Lessons

There has been a shift in the relationship between nonprofit organizations and philanthropists.

Historically, nonprofits took the lead in determining community need, and philanthropy focused on supporting the nonprofit and its program choices. Nowadays, many philanthropists and grant-makers determine the services they believe are most important for the community and then identify nonprofits to supply those services.

Thus, nonprofits increasingly serve as suppliers, and the goal of much philanthropy has been to maximize the service impact of donor money. This focus on leveraging the donor is reflected in grants that require the nonprofit to provide matching funds or provide startup monies for new programs that nonprofits are expected to support independently after a few years.

It has also led to a preference to fund only programs and not to provide operating support. In many cases, it has shifted grants to cost reimbursement rather than cash advances, essentially making the nonprofit the banker for the philanthropy's projects.

This approach was manageable when the economy was strong and nonprofits could develop profit-making programs and tap large numbers of small donors to generate cash to meet donors' terms. Unfortunately, in the economic climate now, the pool of small donors is shrinking and nonprofits are having the same difficulty in earning money as the for-profit sector.

As a result, donors goal to multiply the financial impact of their gifts is being accomplished by requiring that nonprofits provide cash that is increasingly scarce.

To understand the implications of this development, it is helpful to tap some lessons from supply chain management. In a supply chain, the lead company recognizes its dependence on the financial health of its suppliers. In good times, the lead company could compel terms that favored itself over its suppliers, but in difficult times it must be responsive to the financial stress on suppliers if it is to maintain the supply chain.

So, too, must the philanthropic community consider ways to ease the financial strains on nonprofits that are delivering the services the philanthropies want. Particularly helpful are the following steps, which philanthropies can take to improve nonprofits' cashflow and help them remain solvent.

- **Eliminate match requirements:** Grants that require a match cost a nonprofit money. While the nonprofit may have been able to find additional donors in good times, in this environment a match requires a nonprofit to divert existing fundraising from other programs to the program that requires a match. This is the equivalent of a lead company paying a supplier less than the cost of goods supplied. Nonprofits are realizing they cannot afford these matches and they are increasingly turning down such grant awards.

- **Pay the grant award up front:** Nonprofits are rarely well-capitalized, so a grant that pays after services are delivered and costs are documented demands nonprofit capital that may no longer be available. This notion of donor leveraging has the nonprofit finance the service delivery at zero interest. Nonprofits have used reserve funds or bank lines of credit to manage this. Both financing sources are slipping away, creating a cash-flow crisis that may lead nonprofits to have to refuse grants that pay only by reimbursement.

• **Reduce reporting requirements:** The amount of information required by philanthropies, both to apply for and to execute a grant, has increased enormously due to a desire for greater accountability and demonstration of program effectiveness. One cannot dispute the value of accountability, but in difficult times one should examine the administrative burden of specific reporting requirements, particularly for grants that don't pay administrative costs. Much of the cost is caused by having to provide separate, customized reports for each grantor. Since a penny saved is a penny earned, an economical way to help nonprofits would be for grantors to collaborate to reduce the volume, customization, and duplication of required reporting.

• **Include overhead expenses in grant awards:** Any for-profit supplier would reject a contract that did not cover administrative and facility costs because they would eventually go bankrupt. Nonprofits are in a similar position. Heating the building and turning on the lights are essential to any nonprofit's work, yet many grantors will not cover their share of these costs. Many nonprofit failures can be avoided if grants can be modified to cover these essential costs.

• **Make unrestricted grants:** Managing through difficult financial times requires flexibility. For-profit companies have complete flexibility in how they use their funds but nonprofits often must hold the bulk of their cash in restricted form, which means that the cash can be used only for the purpose designated by the donor. Unrestricted grants, or so-called operating support, allow nonprofits to use cash where it is most needed. It is iron-ic that some nonprofits with sufficient cash overall have insufficient unrestricted cash to meet their next payroll.

Nonprofits are the suppliers to the philanthropic commu-nity. In these difficult times, preserving nonprofit suppliers can be the most important step a philanthropy can take.

■ Disclosure: the Good and the Bad

Donors are to nonprofits what investors are to for-profits: people looking for a way to participate in the future of an organization.

In the for-profit world, full and fair disclosure has been deemed so beneficial to investors that the cost to companies is considered worthwhile. As the principle of full and fair disclosure spreads into the nonprofit world we should ask what benefit do donors get and at what cost?

Cost of disclosure

For a long time, the primary standard for nonprofit disclosure was the IRS Form 990 annual nonprofit tax return. This disclosure isn't as widely known by donors, nor is it as carefully filled out by nonprofits.

This is partly because until recently a donor had to visit the offices of the nonprofit or the state attorney general to examine the document. Now a donor can readily see the returns of any U.S. nonprofit by going to www.guidestar. org. The Philanthropic Research Inc.'s *GuideStar* is by far the most extensive and readily accessible source of information on nonprofits.

Unfortunately, the lack of popular appreciation of the breadth and easy accessibility of *GuideStar* information has led many donor advocates to create their own approaches to full and fair disclosure. Examples of this trend are the Better Business Bureau's Wise Giving Alliance reports, the Maryland Association of Nonprofit Organizations' Standards of Excellence and the Greater Kansas City Community Foundation's *DonorEdge*.

The good intentions should be applauded, but these individual efforts are creating a Tower of Babel effect because each approach has its own definition of the appropriate way to profile and identify a responsible nonprofit.

With multiple approaches, a nonprofit needs to customize its responses to each with the effect that the profile it presents can vary, sometimes widely, between the multiple reports. This comes at a cost to each nonprofit with the added disadvantage that the divergent profiles may create mistrust that any of the reports is consistent or reliable.

Nonprofits are understandably reluctant to resist efforts to expand disclosure. Nonetheless, as the for-profit sector benefits from one standard of disclosure by the Securities and Exchange Commission, so the nonprofit sector would benefit by adopting a single standard of disclosure with a single set of definitions of financial and programmatic terms.

Keeping donors informed is a worthy enough goal to warrant better coordination among the IRS and representatives of donors and nonprofits.

Benefits of disclosure?

I admit to being a fan of disclosure and objective evaluation of an organization's effectiveness. But one body of research suggests donors that tolerate excessive administrative costs are more likely to research a new refrigerator than a charity before they write a check and do not respond consistently to measures of the effectiveness of their gifts.

The *Chronicle of Philanthropy* and the *New York Times* have highlighted the work of professor John A. List of the University of Chicago, who studies what motivates donors. He finds that donor decision-making is rational but has little to do with measures of the effectiveness of contributions.

Consider:

- Donors do not respond to opportunities to increase the effectiveness of their gifts. While a challenge gift – giving an additional dollar is matched by a dollar from the challenger – results in additional donations, increasing the match to $2 or $3 for each additional dollar results in no added contributions.

- Donors feel pride by association with the object of their gift, so they are reluctant to study the effectiveness of the charity because that suggests they are not confident the charity is worthy of their pride.

- Donors respond to incentives that have little relation to the value provided by the nonprofit. The least effective method of fundraising is asking for a donation while the most effective is conducting a raffle or lottery. And having a pretty girl ask for the money has more than double the effect on giving as moving from the least effective method (simply asking) to the most effective (the raffle).

Where to start

All this leads to the question of whether we are putting the cart before the horse in asking nonprofits to devote more time, effort, and money to multiplying the ways in which information is disclosed.

Rather, it may be more effective to create a single, rational way to measure the effectiveness of nonprofits and to devote the remaining effort to educating donors on why this method of evaluation is in the donors' best interest. The new disclosure efforts are each legitimate approaches to the right way to look at a nonprofit. But the result of multiple approaches is to raise nonprofits' costs and create a confusing number of right ways without addressing the prior condition for this effort to be worthwhile: Educating donors on how to identify the most appropriate nonprofits to receive their charitable dollars.

VII. WHAT'S NEXT FOR NONPROFITS

Nonprofits, 501(c)(3) organizations, have changed dramatically in the last several decades. The wise nonprofit leader realizes that today's nonprofit sector is big and it is a business that requires hard decisions, strategic governance, and skilled management.

The work of Lester Salamon and S. Wojciech Sokolowski at The Johns Hopkins Nonprofit Employment Data Project has allowed us to see how big the nonprofit sector has become. In 2004 America's nonprofits employed 9.4 million people. If we add to this the 4.7 million full time equivalent workers added by volunteers, nonprofits comprised 10.5% of the U.S. workforce. Wages paid to nonprofit workers almost equaled the wages paid in the finance and insurance industries!

The change in the profile of nonprofits was dramatic in the 2002 recession. While employment in the U.S. economy shrank by 0.2%, nonprofit paid employment grew by 5.1%. This growth wasn't due to nonprofits' mindless ambition; much of this growth was prompted by the continual shift of formerly government-provided services to non-profit-provided services. This change has brought the nonprofit sector a greater prominence in the U.S. economy and in the delivery of public services. Unfortunately, this prominence means that nonprofits are now fully subject to the future twists and turns in the economy and demography of the country.

It also brings a greater awareness that a nonprofit is a business, not a club.

- Nonprofits must be profitable. What makes them different from for-profits is that they always plow their profits back into service improvement.

- Nonprofits must have strong balance sheets and sizable reserves. What makes them different from for-profits is the tension between donor-investor preferences for restrictions on how and when money can be used.

- Nonprofits must continually adapt to a changing market. What makes them different from for-profits is that the customer is not a person but the community, however defined, and its needs.

- Nonprofits must be successful. What makes them different from for-profits is that success in not measured financially but rather by how well they address their mission.

The hard decision-making of a nonprofit must always have a firm anchor in the needs of its community. The preceding chapters of this book have emphasized that great nonprofit leaders do not need to be brilliant if they have good common sense, a passion for what they do, and a laser focus on linking money to mission, mission to action, and action to accomplishment.

Some boards call their members trustees. The word "trustees" evokes an image of white-haired guardians of the past, who meet occasionally in comfortable settings. Nothing could be further from the truth for tomorrow's nonprofit leaders. They will face hard decisions in adapting to new community needs, attracting new supporters, and nurturing leadership in the next generation. They will be successful if they trust their instincts, know their facts, and assemble a board which can continually ground their mission and priorities in the changing environment.

■ Learning to Let Go

The current decade has been difficult for nonprofits. Developments in philanthropy and government funding that began years ago have reached fruition. Cultural shifts have occurred so often that we now have an alphabet soup of generational labels. And then there's the lousy economy.

While dealing with immediate pressures must always take priority, it is useful to look ahead at three challenges that will confront nonprofits in the coming years.

Letting Go

The successful nonprofit of the next decade will need to learn to operate in a permanent state of transition. This will require a new definition of resiliency: Learning to let go of donors, grantors, and services when they no longer support the priorities of the nonprofit's mission.

Donors and grantors increasingly view nonprofits as contractors to carry out programs they define. Their support either is short-term, project oriented or comes with conditions that may create a harmful financial burden on the nonprofit. Whether the donor/grantor chooses to move on because of the former or the nonprofit ends the relationship because of the latter, the resilient nonprofit must plan for a constant churning of its donors and grantors.

Long-term relationships will be more scarce and the nonprofit must become comfortable with proactive marketing for replacement donors and grantors.

The nonprofit must create its own path to financial resiliency. The past two decades have seen three recessions and some sharp investment downturns. Nonprofits will need to value cash reserves more than endowments. They must educate donors to view large reserves as signs of good management rather than as indications that fundraising is unnecessary. And they must educate their own fundraisers that there is a hierarchy in the value of a gift: A dollar of unrestricted cash is worth more than a dollar of restricted cash and a lot more than an endowment gift.

When all else fails, nonprofits will need to come to terms with having an annual review of which services they provide. A sharp focus on current community needs with well-articulated service priorities must be the crucible for regularly identifying which services to keep and which to end. Flexibility will distinguish survival from failure. Non-profits that continually adapt their services will best sustain their core missions.

Make Way for the Next Generation

A few years back the Annie E. Casey Foundation found that 65 percent of the nonprofit leaders it surveyed planned to leave their jobs in the next three years. Moreover, 84 percent were older than 40.

Nonprofits will need to prepare for a substantial change in leadership. They must actively groom today's young professionals to enter both the executive suite and the board-room. Today's young professionals will become tomorrow's primary donor pool. Grooming a sense of volunteerism among young professionals that will evolve into personal philanthropy must become a significant recruitment focus for nonprofits.

The size and significance of the graying baby boom generation places particular urgency on integrating young professionals into nonprofit leadership. Not only must the mission and work environment appeal to them, the method of outreach and communication must adapt to their preferences. Many nonprofits are already integrating social networking into their regular communications.

A web site is now essential for every nonprofit. Web sites must be easy to navigate, always up to date, quick to be found by search engines, and fact-focused. Financial statements, names and titles of staff and trustees, annual reports, program descriptions, and easy links for further information about volunteering, serving on boards, seeking employment, participating in activities – all must use the web site as the first and primary point of contact.

Life in a Fishbowl

Nonprofits have become an essential part of the service delivery system in the United States, particularly in healthcare, social services, and education. That prominence brings increased scrutiny, replacing the quiet obscurity to which many nonprofits have become accustomed.

Excessive executive compensation and tax exemption for over-sized endowments are already in Congressional sights. Publicity and skeptical inquiries will become more common. Nonprofits must adapt their culture and skills to make openness an advantage rather than an annoyance. Openness, transparency, and persuasive communication will become synonymous with nonprofit success.

Transparency will also bring pervasive oversight. Already the familiar IRS Form 990 has evolved from an obscure tax form to the most accessible disclosure about any nonprofit in the United States. Readily available to any donor or employee on www.guidestar.org, the newly revised Form 990 will become a formidable grass roots enforcement tool for effective governance, ethical conduct, responsible management, and mission focus.

How well nonprofits adapt to these trends may well determine whether they thrive or struggle. It is essential that we support the nonprofit leaders who are willing to take the risks that will accompany adapting to these changes.

■ Is Budget Balance the Right Strategy

As nonprofits face another difficult year, too many boards are pressing their executive directors to balance the operating budget. Budget balance is a misused concept of fiscal prudence that dominates state and local government finance, but it is not the norm in for-profit finance and it should not be the norm in nonprofit finance.

A mandate to balance the budget is a crude financial yardstick that is akin to the joke that a broken clock is always right twice a day. The correct yardstick for nonprofit financial management is to be a reliable provider of a service that fulfills a useful need in your community. Being a reliable provider means that you are there when the community needs your services, whether it is during an economic recession or an economic recovery. In financial terms, this is achieved when you are in structural balance.

Structural balance means that you are expected to run operating deficits during economic recessions and you are expected to run surpluses during economic recoveries. Budget balance during recessions usually means denying the needs of the community. Budget balance during recoveries means denying the surpluses that provide the reserves that will stabilize services during the next recession. In neither case is budget balance a wise policy.

This concept of cyclical surpluses and deficits is conventional for for-profit finance. We are not surprised to read reports of corporations losing money for several quarters during a recession. In fact, we expect it. The reason we treat it so routinely is that corporations emphasize retaining earnings and accumulating cash positions that can sustain their business. Layoffs and cutbacks still occur, but it generally occurs at corporations that are financially weak because they did not accumulate sufficient earnings when the economy was strong.

Regardless of these arguments board members may still push for the annual budget proposals to be balanced.

- They believe it is fiscally responsible. The key question is responsible to whom? It is not responsible to the clients and patrons, who are being denied services when cuts are made to balance the budget. And if those services are going to be needed five years from now, the board's responsibility is to have a plan to be able to provide those services five years from now. To do that means the nonprofits needs to be able to survive a prolonged drop in revenues. Cutting services when revenues drop is an admission that the board has not been fiscally responsible in prior years when the economy was strong.

- They believe they must do it to satisfy donors that the nonprofit is well-managed. If running losses during a recession is poor management, then there are very few good managers in the for-profit sector. Rather, the mark of a well-managed organization is the existence of a plan that anticipates risks like declines in sales, grants, or gifts and has assembled contingency plans and reserves that can be tapped if those risks materialize. Cutting expenses because you didn't plan appropriately is not convincing proof of your good management.

- They believe they must do it to avoid running out of cash. The risk of potential bankruptcy or insolvency is not solved by balancing this year's budget. The underlying causes are much more fundamental than the simple math of revenues equaling expenses. If requiring budget balance this year relieves the board of pressure to address the underlying problem, then balancing the budget is actually detrimental; it wins the battle at the peril of losing the war.

The financial crises of this recession should highlight the need for planning ahead so that the opportunities presented by a strengthening economy can be channeled toward preparing for the next recession.

The board's prime fiscal duty to be a stable service provider mandates that it use every recovery to provide for the next recession. To do that, board members should now be acquiring the knowledge and establishing the policies that will enable them to do the following:

- Understand how business cycles can impact both the revenues and the expenses of the nonprofit.

- Understand what types and sizes of reserves are necessary to stabilize services through recessions.

- Educate donors and grantors on the nonprofit's recession planning and their role in helping the nonprofit to build reserves so that it can be a reliable service provider when the next recession arrives.

Balancing the budget is a fiscal short-cut that is rarely a prudent directive. Most of the time, in the context of a well-researched financial plan, a fiscally prudent nonprofit will be running either a surplus or a deficit.

In this recession you may feel you are behind the curve and need to eliminate spending and looming deficits. Just seeking budget balance can be a specious solution to your problems. Instead, be sure any actions you take are buying time for sound planning that will re-establish structural balance and service reliability.

■ Change: When to Move On or Out

The stresses of a weak economy are easily labeled as solely financial, making it possible for nonprofits to miss signals about the continued relevance of their mission to the needs of the community.

Economic disruption should be used as an opportunity to reflect on recent and anticipated changes in the community's needs which your mission addresses. You should take it as given that community needs have changed over the past decade. If your organization is staying ahead of community change, you should have made some of the following adjustments recently:

- Added, dropped, or changed programs.

- Changed how you deliver some or all of your programs.

- Changed the audiences or clients you are serving.

- Changed the service providers with which you work or collaborate.

If your nonprofit has not made similar adjustments, you may be less connected to your community than you think.

Warning signs

The first set of warning signs of an emerging disconnect are recurrent budget cuts or cash crises year after year. The second set is declining clientele, reduced governmental support, diminished fundraising, or more difficulty in attracting volunteers or board members. The second set of cues can be missed because they are also affected by external forces that the nonprofit can blame rather than recognize its emerging marginality.

Quick tests whether the cause is the first or second set is to look at other organizations nearby that address similar missions to see if they are in similar straits. If they seem to be doing better, there may be continued community need for the mission, and the problems of your organization may be internal.

Knowing when to move on

Ideally the chief executive and the board will agree on the situation and on the best response. It takes great skill to manage the potential conflict and disagreement about changing the direction of a nonprofit. Many mistakenly equate respecting a nonprofit's legacy with perpetuating its legacy.

A skilled CEO will demonstrate respect while encouraging change. The CEO should measure his success by his ability to convince the board and staff. Sometimes that may require helping reluctant individuals to recognize that the past they cherish should not be perpetuated and they need to move on.

If a chief executive sees the need for the organization to evolve and cannot convince the rest of the organization, then the choice is to captain a sinking ship or to seek another ship. Perhaps a different chief executive may be more successful in convincing the organization. In all three cases, the chief executive is best served by choosing to move on.

Alternatively, sometimes it is the chief executive who does not recognize the change in the community and who clings to the status quo. This can be a particular problem with a founder of the nonprofit or one who has served so long that he has invested his personal identity so strongly with the organization that he can no longer look at the organization objectively.

If the board does see the need for the organization to evolve but the chief executive does not, then the board has the task of asking the executive to move on. A well-defined succession plan can be a good tool to anticipate the inevitability of change and executive transition and save the organization from the trauma of a board-initiated coup.

Knowing when to turn out the lights

It is more difficult to know when community need has changed so much that the nonprofit should shut down. For-profits have it easier: if they don't make money they should sell, merge, or liquidate.

Non-profits don't have such a simple measure of success or failure. Nonprofit mission is fulfillment of community need. Fulfillment of mission can be elimination of community need, which is a success. Inability to meet a community need is a failure. Nevertheless, in both situations the nonprofit is no longer needed.

Nor do nonprofits have such an obvious set of options as do for-profits. Many for-profits continuously evolve what they make or sell, since the product is less important than the continuation of a profitable company. In sharp contrast, it is not necessarily in the community's interest for a nonprofit to continuously evolve which community need it fulfills.

The existence of one specific nonprofit organization is less important than having community needs be met. The energy that nonprofit staffs and boards might spend on changing their missions in order to preserve the organization is not necessarily the best way to utilize their passion and energy to serve the community. It is okay for a nonprofit to go out of business. It is okay to start a new nonprofit to address a new need. Starting with a clean slate in a new organization can at times be better than trying to retool an old organization into a new one.

It all comes down to meeting the current needs of the community. Clinging to an historic past is honorable but not desirable. If the chief executive, staff, or board member are clinging, it is time for them to move on. If the organization is clinging to its past, it may be time to turn out the lights and raise a toast to an honorable past.

APPENDIX: DO-IT-NOW ACTION RECOMMENDATIONS

■ Governing

✓ Understand how business cycles can impact both the revenues and the expenses of your nonprofits.

✓ Determine how sensitive your nonprofit is to the health of the economy and put together a set of goals to improve your ability to sustain your mission during lean times.

✓ Understand what types and sizes of reserves are necessary to stabilize services through recessions.

✓ Create a timetable of topics for your board meetings in order to create a continual board focus on identification and advancement of long-term goals.

✓ At your next meeting, ask as many questions about good budget results as you ask about unfavorable budget results. Underspending can reflect underperformance, which is not an appropriate way to save money.

✓ Have board members review and agree on their primary duties annually.

✓ Identify the 3 to 5 primary activities of your organization and estimate the principal revenues, contributions, and expenses for each activity.

✓ Make sure that the activities with lower mission priority also have smaller financial losses or larger net revenues.

✓   Review your budget to make sure you don't have "cost efficiencies" that may be undermining the mission-effectiveness of your programs.

✓   Include in each annual budget at least three special initiatives that will advance, strengthen, or sustain your mission.

✓   Prepare your meeting agendas so that the purpose and intended outcomes are clear and the focus is on discussion and decision-making.

✓   Have your finance committee or board treasurer look for excessive compensation, excessive payments, and any payments or investments not consistent with your mission. Study how this is reported in your latest IRS Form 990 filing.

✓   Identify any restrictions on gifts and assets and compare them to your top mission priorities. Take steps to prevent restrictions from diverting your nonprofit's activities from its top mission priorities.

✓   Make sure that your fundraising focuses on sustainability by first building unrestricted cash and reserves to adequate levels before focusing on endowment.

■ Planning

✓ Educate your donors and grantors on recession planning and their roles in helping you to build reserves so that you can be a reliable service provider when the next recession arrives.

✓ Put in place a process to review at least every two years how the community's needs have changed and how your service programs and mission should adapt in response to the changes.

✓ Require that any proposal to expand facilities or services specify the likelihood and future reliability of the new or expanded revenue sources that will fund it.

✓ Look at how your revenues and demand for your services have changed over the last business cycle. How vulnerable is your financial health over the business cycle?

✓ Look at your balance sheet and assess how well you are positioned to sustain services during the next economic downturn: how much cushion do you need and how long can you provide it?

✓ Make sure that you have at least one goal or objective each year that enhances the future sustainability of your services. Do you have a plan to reduce debt, accumulate unrestricted cash, or fund reserves that will enhance your ability to sustain services when lean times return?

✓ Put together a set of goals to advance your mission and a second set of goals to improve your ability to sustain your mission. Have your board adopt them and build them into a multi-year plan.

✓ Determine your need for working capital and your need for separate reserves for emergencies, new program development, and major replacement costs. Have a plan to address those needs over the next 5-10 years and follow it.

■ Managing

✓ Make sure your top priority is to have at least one initiative every year for every long-term goal.

✓ Set up a process to verify throughout the year that spending remains consistent with the priorities the board has set for the year.

✓ Create a summary of what you are doing this year to move toward your long-term goals and regularly communicate this to board members, staff, donors, clients, and patrons.

✓ Make sure you have enough resources available (current assets) to easily pay your bills that are due (current liabilities).

✓ Know what are your unrestricted net assets and whether they are board designated, fixed assets, or readily available for any purpose. Know how or whether each of the assets can be used to pay your bills that are due this year.

✓ Focus on how significant differences between actual and budgeted revenues and expenses may affect your top priorities.

✓ Always have a tickler schedule for when you expect to receive payments on major pledges and grants.

GLOSSARY

501(c)(3) the section of the Internal Revenue Service code that establishes the requirements for tax-exempt status for charitable organizations. This term is often used to refer to an organization which has tax-exempt status.

Accrual basis accounting a method of accounting which records transactions when they occur. Using this method, a pledge of a gift is a transaction recorded when the pledge is made, rather than when the gift is received. A bill is a transaction for payment and is recorded when the bill is received, not paid. Thus, accrual accounting provides a window into some future cash receipts or payments. This future-looking method can require the transaction to be cancelled at a later date such as when a pledge is no longer expected to be received. Pledges over a many-year period are recorded at less than full value under accrual accounting.

Annual audit a procedure performed annually by a certified public accountant to review the organization's financial account and assure the board that the financial statements it receives provide a reasonably good picture of the financial condition of the organization. Audits do not review everything but rather look at a representative sample of transactions to see if they are properly recorded under generally accepted accounting standards. The audit provides opinion letters and a management letter detailing issues of concern to the auditor regarding the organization's operating procedures.

Annual audit meeting a meeting of the full board or the audit committee in which the external audit presents the results to the board of the annual audit. This meeting is a unique opportunity for the board to learn the views and opinions of an objective professional regarding the financial health and operations of the organization.

Asset allocation the distribution of one's investments across various categories such as equities, bonds, treasury securities, and real estate. The asset allocation is the primary determinant of the likely risks and return on investment from an investment program.

Audited statements the end-of-year financial statements of an organization that have been reviewed by an annual audit.

Balancing the budget adjusting the organization's budget so that total revenues equal total expenditures. If the organization has reserves, the adjustments can include adding to or subtracting from reserves. Revenues are difficult to adjust in the middle of a fiscal year so that most mid-year budget balancing efforts are focused on expenditure changes and reserves. When a proposed budget is being reviewed, balancing can include revenue changes such as fee increases or decreases, new fundraising efforts, and grant proposals.

Board designated reserves monies that are set aside for special purposes by board resolution. The resolution can include rules or procedures for adding to or subtracting from the reserves. These rules and procedures can be changed by the board so the financial statements of the organization record these reserves as unrestricted. Reserves are distinguished from endowments by the organization's ability to utilize the entire value of the reserve while it can use only limited portions of an endowment.

Board duties the responsibilities and tasks which the board assigns to itself, as distinguished from the responsibilities and duties of the staff. Generally board duties are limited to strategic and policy issues as opposed to operational duties. In very small nonprofits with few or no staff, board duties may combine with some staff duties, which can be problematic unless the duties are carefully documented in writing.

Board officer a member of the board who has specific responsibilities under statute or by-law. The appointment of officers satisfies legal requirements but all board members share full and equal responsibility for the organization.

Budget a plan for acquiring revenues and incurring expenses for a fiscal year. A budget can be a simple set of estimates of major categories of revenue and expenditure. A budget is most useful if it is based on a specific set of goals and tasks to be achieved during the fiscal year.

Budget balancing strategies policies and plans for adjusting revenues or expenditures, utilizing reserves, investing, or borrowing in order to have resources equal expenses in a fiscal year.

Cash balances investments of an organization that are readily available at their full value. Investments that can be sold at full value within one to three months are viewed as part of cash balances. Bank accounts are considered cash if they can be liquidated without significant penalty in one to three months. A one-year certificate of deposit, for example, would not generally be considered part of cash balances.

Cash basis accounting a method of accounting which records a transaction only when cash is received or disbursed. Cash accounting uses no estimates or adjustments; however, it provides no forward-looking information, such as pledges that will be received or bills that are waiting to be paid.

Cashflow the pattern of cash receipts and expenditures during the fiscal year. Cashflow is the underpinning for having sufficient cash available to meet scheduled expenses, of which payroll and tax obligations are most significant. Positive cashflow refers to periods in which more cash is received than disbursed; negative cashflow refers to periods in which more cash goes out than comes in, reducing cash balances.

Clean opinion also referred to as an unqualified opinion in an audited statement. This boilerplate language by the external auditor is generally as follows : "In our opinion, such financial statements present fairly, in all material respects, the financial position of the Company as of June 30, 2002 and 2001 and the results of its operations, the changes in its net assets, and its cash flows for the years then ended in conformity with accounting principles generally accepted in the United States." Contrast this statement with a qualified opinion, in which the auditor cannot offer such an opinion because the statements do not "present fairly" or they are not "in conformity with accounting principles." A qualified opinion is a major red flag that something abnormal is going on and the board should delve deeply into the auditor's concerns.

Community needs a demand for services that is not completely met by the private or governmental sector. Nonprofit organizations are granted tax-exempt status as an incentive for individuals to contribute funds to the organizations that provide services to address such community needs.

Conservative budget a term often used to describe a budget that intentionally uses low revenue estimates or high expense estimates. This term is a misnomer because this approach to budgeting compromises fulfillment of the organization's mission and is therefore counter to the board's responsibility to conserve the mission.

Continuation and initiatives budget a budget approach that focuses the board's attention on the subset of activities that are intended to change or improve the organization's achievement of its goals, objectives, and mission. Budgeting of ongoing, unchanged, "continuing" activities occurs largely at the staff level only.

Continuation budget the portion of a continuation and initiatives budget that includes the ongoing, unchanged activities from the prior year.

Economic models a series of equations or cells in a spreadsheet that represent the relationships between various activities and their associated revenues and expenses. The main usefulness of models is the effort in assuring that the relationships in the equations or cells are consistent with one another and with the organization's view of how the activities inter-relate.

Endowment an investment account of an organization that is intended to last in perpetuity and which allows only the total investment return to be utilized by the organization. Often the amount and timing of the use of the total return is specified by the original donor or by board resolution.

Endowment draw (see also endowment payout and target rate of return) the amount of total investment return of an endowment that is utilized by the organization in a particular year. The draw may be specified by the original donor or by board resolution. The typical draw is three to five percent of the three-year moving average of the endowment's market value.

Endowment payout (see endowment draw)

Fiduciary a person entrusted with management of, and responsibility for, assets belonging to others. Generally boards of directors of nonprofit organizations are considered to be acting as fiduciaries. A fiduciary can have personal financial liability for mismanagement of the organization. It is common for a nonprofit to indemnify board members and officers and to acquire directors and officers (D&O) insurance to protect the directors' and officers' personal wealth from liability.

Financial planning a multi-year schedule of revenues and expenses that is closely linked to the strategic plan and mission of an organization and which represents an intended approach to provide sufficient resources to sustain that mission over the time period covered by the financial plan.

Financial reports (contrast with financial statements) a set of reports that are prepared for the use of board and/or staff to represent the financial activities and condition of the organization. The most effective financial reports consist of a narrative about progress on the organization's primary goals and objectives for the year with an accompanying table or two of data on that progress.

Financial statements (contrast with financial reports) financial tables that follow the specific definitions and formats required under generally accepted accounting principles (GAAP). Financial statements (as contrasted with financial reports) can be prepared only by certified public accountants (CPAs) in order to receive an unqualified audit opinion (see clean opinion).

Financial strength the ability of an organization to command sufficient resources immediately and over the long term so that it can sustain its mission despite a series of unfavorable events.

Forecasting a plan that assigns specific levels of revenues and expenses to future years. The most important characteristic of a good forecast is that the plan is based on a series of events and activities that are compatible and mutually consistent with each other. It is less important that the level of revenue or expense in any year be an accurate prediction of what revenue or expense actually turns out to be. The board should use a forecast to ascertain if its plans are mutually consistent with each other and whether the plans result in a series of outcomes that are consistent with the mission and priorities of the board.

Initiative a special project that is proposed in a budget to advance a specific goal or objective. An initiative has a specific timetable, set of desired outcomes, and list of required resources that can be easily tracked and managed over the course of the year.

Investment risk the risk that the value of an investment may decline. The cash balances of an organization generally have no investment risk, while endowment funds can have considerable investment risk. Investment risk is related to the return on investment an organization desires and to the asset allocation of the investment portfolio.

IRS Form 990 a mandatory annual filing for any tax-exempt organization except churches and those with less than $25,000 of annual revenues. The form reports on achievement of the organization's mission, allocation of expenditures to each aspect of mission, gifts from major donors, as well as payments to staff, board members, and major vendors and consultants. Widely available on the internet (www.guidestar.org), the Form 990 is increasingly becoming a primary document used by grantors to evaluate the effectiveness and relevance of a nonprofit organization.

Macro level a term used to refer to high-level, organization-wide issues.

Micro level a term used to refer to detailed, operational issues.

Milestones in a timetable for a project or initiative, the dates on which significant stages of the project are expected to be accomplished and to be measurable. Milestones provide the board with an opportunity to inquire objectively about the progress of a project or initiative in an effective and efficient way that does not intrude on the operational role of the staff.

Nonprofit an organization that is tax-exempt (see 501(c)(3)). Nonprofits are distinguished from for-profits by how they spend their profits, not by whether they earn profits.

Permanently restricted a class of gifts in which the donor has set unchangeable rules that limit the organization's ability to utilize the gifts. Restrictions generally specify the purpose for which monies can be spent as well as the amount of money that can be spent in any particular year. Permanently restricted gifts add to the wealth of an organization but they generally are not available for budget balancing purposes.

Profits the amount by which the revenues received from an activity exceed the expenses incurred for that same activity. It is often useful for a board to know which of its activities earn profits and which do not. Most nonprofits will have a sufficient number of profitable activities to provide sufficient monies to support their unprofitable activities and sustain the organization's mission over the years. The calculation of profit can be simplistic or complex depending on how extensively the organization wishes to allocate particular revenues and expenses across more than one activity.

Restricted a term that describes a reserve or endowment that is subject to rules concerning the purpose for which monies can be used or the amount and timing of use of those monies. Restrictions can be unchangeable by the mandate of the donor or they can be changeable at the discretion of the board.

Stability (see sustainability)

Stop-gap financing short-term temporary borrowing during a budgetary crisis that is utilized to continue timely payment of bills during a transition period in which the organization is determining and implementing actions that will return the organization to budget balance.

Strategic planning a multi-year plan which identifies goals and objectives that are necessary to sustain the mission of the organization as well as a set of projects and activities that should lead to achievement of those goals and objectives. A strategic plan should also be accompanied by a financial plan that lays out the specific resources that are needed for those activities and a plan of action to acquire those resources in a timely and reliable manner.

Structural balance a financial plan that is characterized by a stream of revenues that equals the stream of expenditures over a long period of time such as a business cycle. An organization that has structural balance is able to sustain its mission.

Sustainability a desirable quality of a service provided by a nonprofit such that the patron or client utilizing that service can know with reasonable confidence that the service will be available on a reliable basis for the foreseeable future.

Target rate of return in endowment and portfolio investment management, the desired return on investment. The target rate of return is closely related to the asset allocation and investment risk that the organization has chosen. The endowment draw is usually closely related to the target rate of return that is chosen for the endowment.

Temporarily restricted a term that refers to monies that are expected to be available for spending in the current year. Temporarily restricted monies usually are tied to specific expenses such that when the expense occurs the monies are immediately made available to pay the expense. For example, grant monies can be temporarily restricted when the money is already in hand but the organization has not yet provided the service and incurred the expense the grant is funding.

Treasurer the officer of the board who most closely works with the staff responsible for finances and who generally chairs the finance and/or audit committees.

Unrestricted an asset that can be utilized for any purpose desired by the organization. At times the board may still choose to limit the staff's discretion on the use of some unrestricted monies, in which case the unrestricted monies are usually called board designated reserves. Unrestricted assets can be immediately available (unrestricted cash balances) or they can be limited as to the amount and time they are available (unrestricted endowment or board designated reserves).

Unrestricted cash balances assets which are immediately available for any purpose. These assets are usually invested so that there is no investment risk and therefore a lower target rate of return.

Validate execution a limited form of board oversight that seeks to ensure that a high priority activity is meeting the milestones and objectives described in the budget. This oversight occurs on a monthly or quarterly basis and is limited to the criteria for success listed in the budget. It is to be contrasted with management oversight by the staff which pays more frequent and more detailed attention to daily execution by specific staff members.

INDEX

Bold refers to definition

Made in the USA
Charleston, SC
17 January 2011